Paradoxes of Power

Paradoxes of Power

Reflections on the Thatcher Interlude

Alfred Sherman

Edited by
Mark Garnett

ia

imprint-academic.com

Published in the UK by Imprint Academic
PO Box 200, Exeter EX5 5YX, UK

Published in the USA by Imprint Academic
Philosophy Documentation Center
PO Box 7147, Charlottesville, VA 22906-7147, USA

ISBN 1 84540 014 3

A CIP catalogue record for this book is available from the
British Library and US Library of Congress

Contents

The Guardian 10·April·1989

1989 *Guardian* cartoon illustrating back-to-back articles on the 'social market'
economy by Alfred Sherman and Neil Kinnock. Although Kinnock is
undoubtedly looking up to Sherman, readers will notice the
ambiguous nature of the Escher-style drawing [ed.]

Preface

by Rt. Hon. Lord Tebbit C.H.

These essays by 'Alfie' Sherman are highly relevant to the politics of today. His critics include both those who bitterly oppose the ideas he helped to bring to the centre of politics in the late '70s and '80s and those who embrace the ideas but dispute Sherman's claim to have been central in writing the Keith Joseph–Margaret Thatcher agenda. His fans will enjoy the panache with which he still preaches his gospels. Particularly in the early years, Sherman and I scarcely knew each other and we never became close colleagues. We shared an affection for both Margaret Thatcher and Keith Joseph, and our political thinking seemed always in tune. Despite the attacks on all four of us for holding materialistic two-dimensional views, Sherman was extremely aware that free market capitalism is a tool, not an objective — as he constantly demonstrates in these writings. None of us were simply economic liberals, and Sherman is emphatic that 'family and civilised values are the foundation on which the nation and its economy are built.'

Sherman came to his conclusions through intellectual argument from his early Marxist convictions. I can never point to any process by which I reached my own views, similar as they are. In many ways it is as though we mostly inhabited parallel universes, meeting only from time to time, usually in desperate late night speed writing epics in which Sherman's superior typewriting skills gave him a powerful influence on what went in or was left out of the draft.

As an 'ideas' man, as he describes in these essays, Sherman was frequently frustrated by what he says was a simple lack of courage and conviction on the part of us, the politicians. I (and I suspect Keith Joseph and Margaret Thatcher) were often irritated by Sherman's cavalier attitude to the constraints and conventions within which we had to work, but between us at least some progress was made during the 1980s.

Readers of this book will not find it difficult to envisage that earlier Alfred Sherman in his time as a soldier in the Spanish Republican Army. 'Not' as he indignantly corrected a colleague, 'an infantryman. I was a machine gunner.'

And he still is.

Norman Tebbit
House of Lords, March 2005

Editor's Foreword

'I could not have become leader of the Opposition, or achieved what I did as Prime Minister, without Keith [Joseph]. Nor, it is fair to say, could Keith have achieved what he did without the Centre for Policy Studies and Alfred Sherman.'

Margaret Thatcher, *The Path to Power*.[1]

'How MT got herself so thoroughly mixed up with this very clever but twisted man is still a mystery to me.'

George Urban, *Diplomacy and Disillusion at the Court of Margaret Thatcher*.[2]

Thumb through the index of almost any study of the Thatcher years — biographical, scholarly or journalistic — and you will come across the name of Sir Alfred Sherman. The relevant pages include some mixed notices about his abilities and character. 'Talented, if unpredictable' is the unusually tactful verdict of two contributors to a book on the Anglo-American conservative 'revolution' of the

---

[1]   HarperCollins, 1995, 251.
[2]   I.B Taurus, 1996, 70.

1980s.[3] 'Abrasive' is a more common epithet. The late Hugo
Young, while accepting that Sherman was 'an extremist' and
referring to his 'reluctance, in any circumstances, to under-
estimate his own importance', considered him to be
Thatcher's 'chief intellectual provider'.[4] In her memoirs Lady
Thatcher herself pays tribute to Sherman's 'brilliance', the
'force and clarity of his mind', his 'breadth of reading and his
skills as a ruthless polemicist'. She credits him with a central
role in her achievements, especially as leader of the opposition but also after she became prime minister.[5] Some of her
former colleagues, though, are less complimentary. Lord
Howe recalls Sherman as a 'zealot', suggesting that 'good
ideas all too often lost their charm in the light of the zeal with
which he espoused them.'[6]

It is difficult to decide which is the more improbable: the
fact that someone like Sherman became a key prime ministerial adviser, or that someone like Margaret Thatcher was able
to become prime minister. Born in Hackney in London's East
End, the son of a Jewish Labour councillor, until 1948
Sherman was a Communist. Instead of subsiding towards the
Right in easy stages, he soon became an indefatigable free-
market crusader. The present book contains a fascinating
insight into the process of ideological conversion. Sir Alfred

---

[3]   Tim Hames and Richard Feasey, 'Anglo-American think tanks
       under Reagan and Thatcher', in Andrew Adonis and Tim Hames
       (eds) *A Conservative Revolution? The Thatcher-Reagan decade in
       perspective*, Manchester University Press, 1994, 222.

[4]   Hugo Young, *One of Us: A biography of Margaret Thatcher*, Pan, 1990
       edition, 88, 22.

[5]   Thatcher, *Path to Power*, 251.

[6]   Geoffrey Howe, *Conflict of Loyalty*, Macmillan, 1994, 86.

freely acknowledges that he retained much of his Marxist mind-set, even if the ideals were very different. In some ways his odyssey was a help rather than a handicap. As a convert, he knew the best way to encourage a similar change in others. And although he reached this position by a circuitous route, at least he had arrived long before his celebrated coadjutors of the 1970s and early 80s.

Sherman's intellectual equipment gave him a high ranking in the hierarchy of Thatcherite 'gurus'. At the pinnacle were the academic apostles of political and economic freedom, Friedrich von Hayek and Milton Friedman. But Sherman was the middleman who made their message intelligible to the politicians and, through them, to members of the public who wanted an alternative to the post-war consensus. His relationship with Sir Keith Joseph, described below, is probably unique in post-war political history. When they first met in the 1960s Joseph was already a cabinet minister. But he soon learned to defer to Sherman's intellectual authority. After the fall of the Heath Government in February 1974 Joseph needed someone to explain what had gone wrong. At first, Sherman spurned him as someone who had turned out to be 'a lion in opposition but a lamb in government', having been free with taxpayers' money at the Department of Health and Social Security. But this personal rebuff only made Joseph more anxious to win himself a second chance, when he might fulfil his painful sense of public duty.

Thus by the time that the Centre for Policy Studies (CPS) had been established in March 1974 Sherman had begun to act as Joseph's tutor and psychological prop. The relationship has no parallel in post-war British politics. In John Ranelagh's apposite phrase, 'Sherman put a burr under Joseph's saddle'.[7] Without him, Joseph might have undertaken his campaign to convert the Conservative Party to the cause of capitalism, but it would probably have been ineffectual and short-lived. Instead it provoked a debate which went far wider than the confines of the party, and set in train the events leading up to Mrs Thatcher's leadership victory of February 1975.

Sherman himself is sceptical about the extent to which influence 'can be defined, let alone measured or assessed'.[8] But his contribution included two essential ingredients for anyone hoping to bring about a radical change in politics: eloquence, and a sense of certainty. Despite his exposure to some of the more abstruse works of philosophy in a variety of languages, he had the elusive gift of squaring the rhetorical circle. He was not a man for superficial soundbites. But even when the argument made demands on his audience, he could crystallise it in a memorable phrase. His drafting skills, whether for speeches or articles, made a deep and lasting impression on Joseph. Sherman might have been a volatile colleague, but he was also more versatile than his critics imagined. While it suited him to work one-to-one with a politician who normally deferred to his judgement, he could also play a constructive role in the speech-writing team which served the hyper-critical Margaret Thatcher.

But there was one team in public life to which Sherman could never adapt. In Opposition he had furnished Joseph and Thatcher with a hard-hitting critique of the civil service.

---

[7]   John Ranelagh, *Thatcher's People: An insider's account of the politics, the power and the personalities*, HarperCollins, 1991, 174.

[8]   *Guardian*, 29 January 1981.

In his view, bureaucrats were inveterate empire-builders, who would resist radical reform until they had been stripped of the last briefcase and bowler hat. Joseph's conduct at the Department of Industry after the Conservatives returned to office apparently confirmed this analysis. But Joseph was not the only culprit in Sherman's eyes; and Mrs Thatcher's own performance was the more disappointing because he had never questioned her political courage. Although Sherman does not belabour the point, he clearly believes that his own influence waned after 1979 because Thatcher was 'captured' by more orthodox advisers.

The irony here is that most observers believe that Mrs Thatcher 'politicised' the civil service, favouring 'can-do' candidates in her own image over the more traditional type. The accounts conflict because they are the products of polarised perspectives. In Sherman's eyes, the civil service had played a crucial part in creating Britain's post-war problems. If it was not tackled head-on at the earliest opportunity, it would sap the new government's radical impetus. But Sherman's analysis, which owed something to 'rational choice' theory, actually portrayed senior civil servants as deeply *irrational*. If the analysis was true, the denizens of Whitehall would have been eager to take on additional responsibilities at the very time that orthodox post-war ideas about the virtues of state activism were falling into general disrepute. This mentality was brilliantly portrayed in the contemporary sitcom *Yes, Minister,* but it had little relevance to reality.

In practice, civil servants knew that they would have to reach some kind of accommodation with the incoming Thatcher Government. But Sherman, for his part, was not prepared to compromise. He and his 'outsider' allies, John Hoskyns and Norman Strauss, had planned carefully for a radical reforming government. For the supporters of the post-war consensus the first Thatcher Government was quite radical enough. But by 1983 Hoskyns, Strauss and Sherman had either departed or become disillusioned, because in their view the government had been too timid in its approach both to institutions and to policies.

Sherman never minimised the distance between his outlook and that of the average British MP, famously complaining that he was a 'man of ideas fallen among party politicians'.[9] But this is not to say that he was a lion in opposition and a loose cannon in government. His greatest direct service after 1979 was the appointment of Jurg Niehans, on his own initiative, to investigate a monetary policy which was palpably failing. In this respect, at least, Sherman was actually more pragmatic than Treasury ministers. But, as Mrs Thatcher put it on a later occasion, 'Advisers advise; ministers decide.' Government advisers are allowed to have an agenda of their own; but they must keep it to themselves until they find that their objectives coincide with those of their political masters. Even in the Niehans incident Sherman was driving forward his own agenda; and (as Machiavelli could have warned) prudent advisers should never try to prove themselves right when the official policy is perverse.

As Sherman recounts below, the precise reasons for his departure from the inner Thatcher circle are unclear, and it is

---

[9]   Quoted in Richard Cockett, *Thinking the Unthinkable: Think-tanks and the economic counter-revolution 1931-1983*, HarperCollins, 1994, 235.

unlikely that the prime minister herself wanted him to go. But it was somehow fitting that events within the CPS provide part of the explanation. From the outset Sherman had been the animating spirit of an organisation which lacked resources; but he had never been allowed to control it. Almost certainly he was obstructed by anti-semitism, and his Marxist past was also held against him. But probably none of this would have counted had he been what William Hazlitt sneeringly called 'A Good-Natured Man'.[10] Margaret Thatcher wanted to re-write the political rule-book; but Alfred Sherman wanted to see it burn. After his protégée had been re-elected in 1983 she could feel part of a new and altered Establishment, with no reason to retain those among her supporters who were instinctively suspicious of anything that smacked of complacency. Whether or not Britain is better off for the change, on an objective review of events since 1983, is for the reader to decide.

Sherman's departure from the inner circle of Thatcher's advisers left him with a dilemma. Sensing that the Conservative 'revolution' would be incomplete without additional impetus, he had a strong desire to maintain his contribution to the debate on Britain's future. But in order to establish his credentials as a commentator, he had to remind readers of his part in the 1974–9 period. As a result, he left himself vulnerable to the charge that he had overstated his role. Once he had departed from the scene critics like George Urban could accuse him of egotism, while simultaneously regretting that Margaret Thatcher had allowed herself to get 'so thoroughly

[10] William Hazlitt, 'On Good Nature', *The Round Table*, Everyman's edition, 1936,100–5.

mixed up' with such a man. It is fairly easy to read between
the lines of the various accounts. Sherman's influence during
the formative years of 'Thatcherism' was at least equivalent
to that of Sir Keith Joseph. But the latter's role has never been
disputed, largely because he was incapable of making personal enemies. Whenever the 'abrasive' Sherman caused
offence, he gave someone a new reason for both deploring
and belittling his contribution.

The treatment of Sherman after his enforced departure
from the CPS reminds us that intellectuals rarely prosper
when they stray into politics. Sherman was not tortured like
Machiavelli, or impeached like Francis Bacon; but his fate
was similar to theirs in that he enjoyed a glimpse of power
through his own endeavours, and was forced to recognise the
limitations of unaided brain-power when favour was
snatched away. For good or ill, Sherman's career reinforces
the old cliché about prophets without honour. Whatever the
merits of his economic arguments, his advocacy of 'joined-
up' government, overseen by a fully-fledged Prime Minister's Department, should strike the reader as unusually far-
sighted. Sadly, although government coordination has been
trumpeted since 1997, the reality is as distant as it was back in
1979.

Since the end of his formal connection with Lady
Thatcher's inner circle, Sir Alfred Sherman has retained his
gift for getting into controversial company. He remains a pro-
lific writer. The main text of this book has been compiled
from a large number of manuscripts which were composed in
Sir Alfred's favoured essay form. As editor, I have regarded
this process of distillation as my main task; the explanatory
footnotes have been minimised in the expectation that read-

ers will already be aware of most of the personalities and events. I should add that although my own perspective on the Thatcher years could hardly be more different, I wholeheartedly agree with Sir Alfred's prediction that a collaboration on this project might be both fruitful and fun. We have also been fortunate in our choice of publisher; our thanks go to all at Imprint Academic, particularly the ever-resourceful Keith Sutherland.

Introduction

A s the sub-title suggests, these are reflections, not a systematic narrative or an attempt at a final assessment of Margaret Thatcher's contribution to British politics. They are also 'partial' in the sense that I was a partisan during the period which I describe. But within these obvious limits I hope to provide an objective account of events and of my own part in them.

I was a participant in the process which brought Margaret Thatcher to the top of the greasy parliamentary pole, and helped to sustain her there during her early years. If Mrs Thatcher's opponents were to be believed, I was a dominant influence on her thinking. My answer was that I only wished they were right.

In any case, how is influence to be defined, let alone measured or assessed? Would it not take a competent historian half a working lifetime to attempt the task? Does 'influence' in this respect mean to change someone's thinking, or merely to provide intellectual support for someone whose ideas are already formed?[1]

Whatever influence I really did exercise over Mrs Thatcher in Opposition and during her first Government, I remain proud of it: it was my greatest achievement in life. But it obviously means that I lack detachment; and I also lack the scholarship to provide a balanced assessment of the achievements and ultimate failures of those years. I seek to derive wider lessons from the experience, which should be a major objective in historiography. I also want to explore the interface in Mrs Thatcher's story between the accidental/incidental and what Hegel called 'necessity'.

I designate Mrs Thatcher's stint as party leader and prime minister as an 'interlude', because what followed was largely a return to what had gone before. But not quite: she did leave a legacy. Her departure also bequeathed an ideological vacuum, which remains to be filled on the Tory side. Until it comes to terms with the Thatcher legacy, and incorporates it into its present stance, the party will be hard pressed to face the future. By turning their back on her, Conservatives cut themselves off from their own history.

The politico-economic context, though it looms large, is only part of the story. There is also the sheer romance of it, which will remain alive for generations of readers in the wider world who may know little of late twentieth-century British politics and care even less. A woman from the provincial lower-middle class, without family connections, oratorical skills, intellectual standing or factional backing of any

---

[1]   AS, 'Confessions of a man of ideas fallen among party politicians', *Guardian*, 29 June 1981.

sort, established herself as leader of a great party which had represented hierarchy, social stratification and male dominance.

Having won the leadership and retained it through early vicissitudes, she flowered and became a dominant world figure, a name to be conjured with — the only British politician whose name has become an 'ism'.[2] She took her party from behind to win three general elections, and would have won a fourth had she not neglected her power base — the parliamentary Conservative Party, which had never felt at ease with her.

What were the personal qualities which underlay these achievements? Leadership combines personal chemistry and institutional arrangements conferring power and legitimacy. In short, leaders are both born *and* made. Margaret Thatcher began as an elected leader without much in the way of control over the levers of power or the loyalties of her colleagues and the party machine.

Much of her history concerns her relationship with power groups and her gradual acquisition of personal ascendancy over the party membership. This strengthened her hand, yet did not save her when the fateful 1990 leadership election took place, partly because she made no effort to exploit it. Thatcher's 'chemistry' remains a challenge to commentators. By way of contrast with Churchill (an historic figure and a scion of an aristocratic house), and Sir Alec Douglas-Home

---

[2] Commentators have spoken of 'Blairism' and even 'Majorism'; but this merely suggests that after Mrs Thatcher no prime minister seemed to be complete without an 'ism' of their own [editor's note].

(who excited genuine reverence), she started with the least and acquired most. Again, however, the Thatcher 'cult of personality' was not enough to save her.

The ever-present question is how much a leader can achieve under the British system of parliamentary democracy, which grew up spontaneously over time, reflecting immemorial institutions and national temperament. The nineteenth and twentieth century Conservative version of leadership bore comparison with the version of tribal chieftainship described in Sir James Frazer's *The Golden Bough*. During his tenure, the chief was all-powerful. But at a given stage he was killed by the tribe. Since the third Marquess of Salisbury in 1902 only the departures from office of Baldwin and Churchill could reasonably be described as 'voluntary'. Baldwin departed amid plaudits, but was subsequently excoriated. By 1955 control had long been slipping from the hands of the elderly, ailing Churchill, who wished to postpone for as long as possible the Buggins'-turn succession of Anthony Eden, whom he mistrusted.

The leadership principle tends to be taken for granted and treated as a constant. In fact it has a history — beginnings, growth and new crises. It emerged as the monarch no longer ruled through his ministers; the leader took his place. It took time for the parties to realise that there could be only one leader, not one for each House of Parliament.

Leadership counted for less so long as the state appropriated and spent only a few per cent of national income. As that proportion grew, and various dimensions of government activity needed coordination, one man had to keep all the balls in the air and the leader's role came to dominate.

The choice of Conservative leader had traditionally been consensual, which meant that the leader inherited his policies from his predecessors and colleagues. Conflicts of principle (eg the Corn Laws and Imperial preference) were the exception. Lord Salisbury described his technique as drifting downstream in a punt while fending off the banks. Significantly, his spell as party leader (1881–1902) coincided with a period of relative national decline.

The leader had to be more than just *primus inter pares*; some magic and mystery are necessary components, together with the skills of chairman, chief executive and spokesman. The leader had to be a star, yet to begin shining only once he had reached the top. The leader lacked machinery or techniques for moulding opinion within his party or the wider public. The Conservative Research Department (CRD — founded under Baldwin in 1929) was designed to serve the cabinet, or shadow cabinet, with a greatly enhanced role in opposition when the civil service was not available to help.

When Thatcher led the Conservative opposition the CRD worked against her, promoting the claims of James Prior. William Whitelaw persuaded Mrs Thatcher to overlook this treachery in order to avoid provoking bad blood. Meanwhile the Conservative Political Centre (CPC), the party's publishing arm, had limited reach. Party members and Tory voters were exposed to the same media and other influences as their fellow citizens.

In short, the leader could ride waves, rather than making them. The institution of consensual leadership suited periods of slow incremental reform, but was an obstacle to rapid, large-scale changes of direction. The abolition of the consensual system, bound by informal conventions, was to have unforeseen side-effects which are still working themselves out four decades later. Under the old system, a displaced leader took his fate with a good grace and usually served loyally under his successor; even Neville Chamberlain, after his humiliating ejection in May 1940, became a reliable supporter of Winston Churchill.

The situation changed after 1963, when Douglas-Home 'emerged' as leader and prime minister in succession to Harold Macmillan. In protest at the role of a so-called 'Magic Circle' in promoting Douglas-Home rather than R.A Butler, Iain Macleod and Enoch Powell refused to join the new cabinet. Powell once explained his reasons to me at length, but I found them unconvincing.

If Powell and Macleod had not acted, who knows? Margaret Thatcher might have remained among the 'mute inglorious Miltons' of the Conservative Party. In response to the damaging mutiny of two dynamic ministers, a new system was introduced which meant that future leaders would be chosen through a secret ballot of MPs. This reform intruded electioneering for the leadership into the parliamentary party. Electioneering involved not only ideas and policies but also promises and pledges, *quid pro quos* and obligations. Like any form of electioneering, it was not limited to the election itself, but preceded it and persisted afterwards. Whereas the old system was (usually) a unifying factor, the new system proved to be inherently divisive — even more so when it was reformed in 1974, to make it easier to mount a challenge. It made the party amenable to takeover but correspondingly difficult to lead; the principle of election implies the possibility of de-selection. The symptoms were not immediately recognised. But many of Thatcher's difficulties arose from it, rather than from her style or policies.

In the past, leaders had been well known before reaching high office. This held good for Edward Heath, who had risen through the hierarchy after distinguished war service and highly-praised service as Chief Whip. Margaret Thatcher was the first virtually unknown leader — less prominent within the party even than Andrew Bonar Law, the so-called 'Unknown Prime Minister' (1922-3).

The rush to understand her was hurried and superficial. I knew her better than most, but was inhibited by our relationship from going public. I was always aware of the limitations of my understanding. By definition, leaders elude the understandings of the led. The apparel of leadership creates the illusion of distance and distorts the picture. Commentators with less knowledge and therefore fewer inhibitions used her as a dummy on which to hang their ideas, ascribing to her their own thoughts and aspirations. In particular, she was seen as a parrot for the ideas of intellectuals like Friedrich von Hayek and Milton Friedman, who at most provided reinforcement for principles she already held instinctively.

Mrs Thatcher was a practical illustration of a distinction drawn by the Spanish political philosopher José Ortega y Gasset: she was a woman of beliefs, and not of ideas (beliefs, in his view, being the more important).[3] Her greatest intellectual gift was for simplification — useful for a politician, but

---

[3] Ortega y Gasset, *Ideas y creencias* [*Ideas and Beliefs*], Espace Calpe, 1940. See Andrew Dobson, *An Introduction to the Politics and Philosophy of José Ortega y Gasset*, Cambridge University Press, 1989, 117-8.

hardly decisive. In the eight years that we worked closely together I never heard her express an original idea or even ask an insightful question. She has left no memorable sayings, apart from one quoted against her out of context.[4] But she saw life in primary colours. The unmistakable distinction between right and wrong, the need to live within one's income, patriotism — they all tripped off her tongue.

I remember early in our acquaintance taking her to dinner at the Reform Club with two leader writers from the *Daily Telegraph*, John O'Sullivan and the late T.E Utley. The following day Utley remarked 'What a banal woman!' It was difficult for me to explain why this was wrong; Utley himself in time revised his view, after the benefit of further acquaintance.

I found it hard to tell at any given time how far she was acting naturally, and how far she was putting on a show, which is second nature to politicians. Remember, she was a barrister and had been a cabinet minister; she knew how to appear sophisticated. I was reminded of Peel's dictum that a prime minister ought to be 'an uncommon common man'. Sometimes it was possible to see that she was putting on an act of 'ordinariness' and that the real Margaret Thatcher was miles away.

But one could not always be sure. Kesteven and Grantham Girl's Grammar School was not Winchester. I noted her ability to relate to people and to empathise with them, which was

---

[4]   'There is no such thing as society', taken from a 1987 *Woman's Own* interview. One might also cite 'You turn if you want to: the Lady's not for turning', from her speech to the 1980 Conservative Party conference; but that phrase was not her own [editor's note].

not generally shared by Conservative politicians for all their superficial *bonhomie*. This was also a function of her position as leader, filling a space in peoples' consciousness.

Her early life showed no indication of a brilliant future, only competence and a capacity for hard, disciplined work, and of course ambition. At Oxford she did not shine. She was politically active in a run-of-the-mill way, but she generated no prophesies. With her nose to the grindstone she secured a second-class degree, and left for a middling first job as a research chemist. Later she made a good marriage, which allowed her to go in for the Bar and afford a nanny for her two children. She had taken elocution lessons, and passed as an archetypal Tory lady in twin set and pearls. Having fought a hopeless seat on two occasions before her marriage, in 1958 she was eventually adopted for Finchley, in face of fierce competition.

What had led her selectors to choose a woman — a rarity in those days — and this one in particular? Did the upwardly-mobile Jewish population of that North London suburb, many of them first-generation Conservatives, empathise with her rather than with the standard Tory seat-seekers of the time? Did they see something even then, which the rest of were to discover much later? Or was it that she impressed them as 'safe'?

With her qualification at the Bar, a safe seat and a sound family life, she was marked out for promotion in a party which always needed one token woman in a prominent (if not powerful) position. Not very clubbable and with no reputation as a thinker, two years after her election at Finchley she was made under-secretary at the Ministry of Pensions where she impressed as a reliable parliamentary performer. She made little public impact during the years in opposition between 1964 and 1970, although in 1968 she was chosen to give the annual Conservative Political Centre lecture at the party conference — a mark of some distinction. By that time she was a member of the shadow cabinet led by Edward Heath. Her speech showed some stirrings of what was to come, but at the time no one thought it particularly noteworthy.

Compared with most Conservative party leaders or leading figures, she was an entirely political animal — and a party-political animal at that. She did not paint, write, make music, lay bricks or pretend to follow football teams. She did not compose her own speeches or articles. But already she could express conviction, in the voice of her father Alfred Roberts — Methodist lay preacher, alderman and shopkeeper.

Any study of her must come back to her father, whose voice was transmitted and transmuted through his daughter. Unlike the general run of Conservative politicians who are shaped by residential public schools, she was influenced much more by home than by school, which was for weekday learning. She attended church services regularly, worked in the shop, met her father's associates. Grantham was her world — to an extent unimaginable nowadays in the age of the motor-car and the internet.

Political biography traces the interaction of personality and circumstances. When we ask what kind of woman could have risen so far from such inauspicious beginnings, we must correspondingly ask what kind of country lent itself to dominant leadership by an outsider who blew in like a hurricane, undertaking to innovate in the name of tradition, and renew in the cause of conserving? The Thatcher interlude is a crucial part of contemporary British history — political, social and economic, but also spiritual and psychological. Were it not for a deep crisis in Conservatism — political and governmental — she could never have come near the starting line. Without a similar crisis within the Labour Party at that time, she could not have won an election and then sustained her parliamentary majority. Without a mood of desperation in Britain, three decades after the Second World War, as many hopes gave way to frustration and despondency, neither the Conservatives nor the general public would have countenanced such a vigorous new broom.

Today it seems that the impulse of the mid-seventies which expressed itself in the 'new right' or Thatcherism appears to have run its course, though the ills which gave birth to it are still with us. A disconcerting thought arises: the 'new right' was a product of the early post-war years, a reaction against the 'consensus' or 'Butskellite' approach, and may have died with it. Mrs Thatcher's powers were limited in scope and time. The new right remained a minority among Conservatives, with little purchase beyond their immediate milieux. True, the socio-Keynesian certainties of the early post-war decades have lost their credence. But there are probably still more Marxists in Oxford than in Moscow and more class warriors on the Clyde than the Neva, even if their faith has declined, while 'tax and spend' retains its inherent public appeal. The state sector survived a measure of privatisation. In education, comprehensivisation has not been reversed, though its original purpose has been forgotten. The millions of unemployed and non-employed, living off disability benefits, other forms of welfare, crime and the black economy, continue to do so.

There have been efforts to change the lie of the land. But change was not necessarily welcome to those affected. When Enoch Powell received his first ministerial appointment (1955), the state accounted for a quarter of Gross Domestic Product (GDP). When the Conservatives handed over government in 1997, the proportion had risen to over forty percent. Yet who had benefited?

When the public sector embraces such a high proportion of the population, drawing wages, salaries, pensions, benefits, and so-called 'tax-credits', obstacles to change are inbuilt. There are limits to the scope for revolution from above, while the civil service and the universities retain their stranglehold. There have been no consistent pressures for old-style revolution from below, except among the Celtic fringes, or from public services which seek 'more, regardless'.

Intellectually, the new right has swept the board as far as economic theory is concerned. The Institute of Economic Affairs (IEA) and Adam Smith Institute (ASI) dominate economic thinking in Britain; the think-tanks linked to Labour, like the Institute of Public Policy Research (IPPR) and Demos differ only at the margin.

But that intellectual eminence has not been transmuted into economic policy, and there is no prospect of this happening, so long as public expenditure is widely seen as an unqualified good. Smithian certainties which seemed to us poised to dominate ideas and policies alike have once again been sidelined at government level.

Not only does the Thatcher revolution appear to have run its course; the quest for an intellectually-disciplined policy framework, whether of 'right' or 'left' has given way to the more familiar personalist and factionalist policies of the past.

We are back to where we started.

Chapter 1

The Outsider Inside

As the theory of relativity has it, the observer is part of the picture. So it would be worth including a few words about myself, to help explain why I was able to play an important role for a short but vital period in the political life of our country.

I could call myself a child of the twentieth century, born in London's East End in November 1919, a year after the Armistice which ushered in the new century and swept away the debris of the old — good and bad alike. My family were poor Jewish immigrants from the Russian Empire. Although turn-of-the-century Jewish immigration numbered little more than a hundred thousand by the time the Aliens Act (1905) attenuated it, the writings of the time did not give that impression. Jews were then encouraged to fit into their new home in all but their separate religious observances, and to work out their own salvation.

My first way of doing this was to 'join the proletariat', as I saw it. I became a communist. The growth of Marxism from the musings of an obscure mid-nineteenth century German intellectual to a major world movement and quasi-religion has been amply documented and commented on. But questions remain unanswered. Why did Marxism and communist dictatorships enjoy so much adulation — and sometimes even more — among educated classes in the West, long after their spell had been broken *in situ*, where only time-servers supported them?

We inherited a bleak world after 1918; the optimism generated by the Victorian age was dissipated. We sought new utopias. For myself, there was another dimension. A few decades ago, studies told us what we already guessed: half the communists in both the USA and the UK were Jewish, out of a negligible population base. These were not the poorest of Jews, who for the most part remained traditional and religious. By contrast we were a transitional phenomenon, having lost much of our inherited Jewish identity and values without fully acquiring and internalising British ones. We Jews had been formed by three thousand years of religious culture: 'I shall make you a nation of priests'. Our atheism or agnosticism had a strong religious flavour. When we deserted the God of our fathers, we were bound to go whoring after strange gods, of which socialism in its various forms was a prominent choice.

From its inception, communism was largely Jewish. But eventually it turned on the Jews. The parallel with Christianity is strong, to a lesser extent with Islam. Jesus was a Jewish religious reformer who cared nothing for the Gentiles. After his crucifixion as a Jew, some of his partisans mythologised him, giving him Godlike attributes which he had always rejected, being in the prophetic tradition. Then Paul posthumously revised his remit — from Jewish salvation to a universal mission, to reach all of mankind. This is turn marginalised the Jews, who were no longer a chosen people but rather a deicidal sect. They were left with three choices over the centuries: to Christianise; to retain their faith at whatever cost; or to seek new *modus vivendi*. But, for most of the time, the Jews remained on the margins of society, awaiting the coming of the true Messiah. Jews carried with them, as a snail carries its shell, the prophetic promise of a revolution in human nature, when 'the wolf would life down with the lamb'. Socialism was the latest of these dreams, which during the twentieth century turned into a nightmare. The nature of the Czarist regime in Russia had been such that Jews could be forgiven for taking the Bolshevik claims at face value. But they could not be forgiven for their slowness in eventually coming to terms with the squalid reality.

My service in the Spanish Civil War in the International Brigades could be said to have broadened my horizons. The Brigades, of which over a third were Jews, changed the course of history in that they gave the Spanish Republic a breathing space to organise itself militarily after the *coup* and survive for three years, depriving the Franco regime of the legitimacy which rapid victory would have accorded it. A contingent of natural rebels created a disciplined force, behind which the Republic's institutions firmed up. It gave substance to airy ideas of internationalism. It gave people like me a sense of belonging which British society had failed to do, and all the greater a sense of loss after its collapse.

I can add little to existing accounts of the war, which has been lavishly treated in literature and historical studies. Because I spoke fluent Russian and Spanish, I was often called upon to interpret for generals and other visitors, and shared with them a vision of the uncertainties of a war which we were well on the way to losing. While the conflict proceeded, we saw ourselves privileged to stand at the crossroads of history, at whatever personal cost. Our valuation was widely accepted. In retrospect, we were betrayed by Stalin, and eventually used as a bargaining counter with the Germans. But the three hundred at Thermopylae had been similarly betrayed and destroyed, yet their sacrifice resonates throughout history and has inspired generations. We minor Spartans glorified in our role. Seventeen is a good age for a soldier.

Those of us who dealt with Spaniards at first hand saw a new world. Our interlocutors were so different from the semi-suburban dross among whom we had grown up. Naturally, almost all the people we met were Republicans, so we may have formed a partial picture. But even after his victory, Spain never became 'Franquist'. For years after the Spanish war the resonance remained. Writing in the nineteen-twenties, Ortega y Gasset observed that when everything good is possible, the worst is also possible.[1] Stalin realised this, and produced one of the least successful regimes in history (though for years the most highly esteemed by those who did not experience its failures). Why should it have occurred at all? Was Stalin unavoidable? At what point did

---

[1]   *Meditaciones del Quijote* (1914) [*Meditations on Quixote*, Norton, 1984].

the Spanish civil war become inevitable? And once it had become inevitable, could it have been anything less than a world war by proxy?

De-communisation reached me eventually, as it did most believers sooner or later. With me it entailed a synthesis of two realisations: first, that the communist dream was an example of self-deception beyond repair, and secondly that socio-economic processes had an autonomy of their own which could be influenced, up to a point, by intervention based on human understanding — but only within the limits set by the nature of the social process. It is worth noting that when Marx and his contemporaries spoke of 'alienation', they meant that the social process was alienated from its participants and appeared to them as external reality with which they had to grapple, not *vice versa*. This remains closer to the original Marxist thesis than the 'voluntarist' megalomania of Stalin, Mao-Tse Tung, Pol Pot and Ho Chi Minh, with their slogan 'Let politics take control!' implying the supremacy of the Will.

My experience was nothing out of the ordinary — communist movements have a high turnover. Communism as religion-substitute has the disadvantage of susceptibility to judgement by results, unlike 'the bourne from which no traveller returns'. My belief that there must be a better way forward survived the break with communism. In a few post-communist years I gained some standing as a commentator on Soviet and Balkan affairs, including a stint as *Observer* correspondent in Belgrade, where I was to discover that communism, however 'heroic', was incapable of developing a broad enough popular base to permit democracy or any meaningful form of suffrage.

Study of Yugoslavia also gave me cause for thinking that a command economy, widely canvassed the world over as a step forward, was no more rational than the supposed 'anarchy' of the free market. It took time for socialists and other *bien pensants* to measure up to this realisation, indeed many have yet to take it on board. But I also learned that this should not lead to market worship. The rationality of the market is genuine, but it constitutes the lowest form of rationality. In time, mankind should aspire to do better. Mankind must attempt to control its social environment no less than its material surroundings. This calls for greater intellectual sensitivity and self-discipline. The problem seems impossible to tackle, until the detritus of socialism and statism have been swept away. But the 'New Right' never became ideologically capitalist in the way that socialists are socialist. The world is too big to fit into a single ideology. Population growth and distribution, migration, uneven development between countries, ethnic interactions, climate change, family breakdown, changing sexual mores, the drug culture, technical change, tides of religious upheaval, are not necessarily self-regulating. Market forces are simply part of a far wider pattern, 'sent to try us'.

Did my apprenticeship within the communist movement contribute to my later activities with Keith Joseph and Margaret Thatcher? Probably. For many years, I regarded my communist decade as time wasted, a misadventure to be sloughed off. But on second thoughts, it can be regarded as an essential ingredient in the mix which prepared me to take a hand in key political events in the 1970s. As a communist, I learned to think big, to believe that, aligned with the forces of history, a handful of people with sufficient faith could move mountains. I took nothing for granted, but sought explanations as to 'why'. I questioned words and the assumptions which hid behind them.

During the Second World War, I learned Arabic and gained useful insights into the Arab and Moslem mind-set. I became aware of the continued relevance of national and religious questions; contrary to Marxist assumptions, these factors transcend economics as major historical forces. When I was born, the word 'British' had clearly understood meanings, and religion was understood as a staple of identity. These lessons have been comprehensively unlearned. Conservatives shirked such questions.

Though Conservatism generally considers itself to be pragmatic, and is regarded as such, there is a strong element of utopianism in it and an even greater utopian potential. It envisaged the rule of moderation, common sense, justice and precedent, which is much to hope for. The 'New Right', mainly converts from communism or socialism, had their own version of utopianism, and structured thinking to accompany these great expectations. This gave us a weight disproportionate to our numbers. We saw inherent possibilities and potentialities, and endeavoured to realise them. Our novelty lay not in our ideas, but in our degree of commitment. While the Conservative Party was in the doldrums it lent an ear to these aspirations; back in the saddle, Conservatives of the old school became less receptive.

It was the traditional Conservatives who had changed during the twentieth century, partly as a result of the bloodletting of two world wars, partly as a concomitant of the expansion of the role of the state and the loss of empire. To think of them as 'appeasers' or 'defeatists', as we often did in the 1970s, might be less than fair to their motives. They saw themselves as making the best of a bad job. Their morale had been undermined, and they swam with the tide. Even the most intellectually-distinguished among them had compromised their basic aims and *raison d'etre* in order to facilitate their survival as a party of government. Values and historical objectives became disposable: electoral success changed from means to end. The 'converts', by contrast, brought with them combativeness, elements of messianism and a cosmology which left room for the role of ideas.

The role of religion in Conservatism deserves closer inspection. Britain is still a Christian country, but less so than it was. During Mrs Thatcher's time in office residual deference towards the monarchy caused tensions within the party; Conservatives sat with a photograph of Her Majesty the Queen on one wall and Margaret Thatcher on the other, hoping uncomfortably that they would never have to choose between them. But for generations, the Tories were a 'Church and King' party, in that order. Conservatism meant respectability, less an ideology than an identity, a bowler hat against a cloth cap. It stood for the status quo as the natural order of things. Part of that order was the Church as an institution rather than a system of belief. Religion and politics were intertwined. There is still no agreement on why British politics became so de-theologised. Is it because religion failed to keep up with science, or because society became less religious for other reasons? In the post-war period what was left of Christianity was appropriated by socialists — clerical or lay — without Conservative objection or resistance. I personally questioned this, on grounds of intellectual history. Christianity — I argued — was more than just a religion; it was a culture, a civilisation. British society and politics were Christian.

The de-theologisation of British politics, not necessarily matched in Europe or the USA, left a vacuum. Many Tories simply lived in this vacuum. Towards the end of the opposition period I urged restatement of Christian culture and the Protestant ethic within a Conservative framework. Margaret Thatcher was enthusiastic. Together with Simon Webley and the late T.E Utley, I produced a talk which Mrs Thatcher gave at St Lawrence Jewry in London.[2] Things went wrong. The *Daily Telegraph* sent a reporter to cover the speech, but for whatever reason failed to publish it. The *Times* had gone on strike. So the initiative was lost. Mrs Thatcher's colleagues were lukewarm or worse. They preferred leaving religion to the clergy, not noticing that the Church had become increasingly hostile: it had 'abandoned faith in the next world for certainties about the third world', as someone remarked. Blair eventually exploited the vacuum. But he did not fill it. Christian belief and charity is far from being restored, along with the Christian resignation that reconciled all to their lot.

That the Conservative Party today is in crisis and has been for some time needs no demonstration. Yet for long periods it enjoyed parliamentary majorities. They were based on sentiment rather than logic. Conservatism did not argue, but pronounced. The subsequent growth and dominance of the argumentative society took it by surprise. It was less inclined to argue its case than to compromise and seek popular slogans and panaceas. A side-effect of this characteristic was the party's structural inability to criticise and purge itself of past

[2]   March 1978.

errors. The party could do no wrong: hence there could be no errors to correct. Job-saving and short-term job-creation were hailed as unquestioned goods, as were labour imports — irrespective of social costs. The New Right sought to remedy these shortcomings; we had some early successes but many more failures. We were, after all, trying to reform society both in theory and practice. I tried to institutionalise reform in my work at the CPS, but was met with inbuilt resistance to intellectual reorientation. After almost ten years, I was sent packing.

Chapter 2

Keith Joseph and The Centre for Policy Studies

Human affairs do not run along straight lines. Incident and accident interact with what Hegel called 'necessity', to create new patterns which are not only unpredicted, but unpredictable. None of the great figures, mostly malevolent, who stride across the pages of twentieth-century history were predicted; and even when they achieved power the likely course of their careers was totally, and often tragically, misconceived. The wild card which launched Margaret Thatcher on her career as Pretender to leadership from a relatively humble position in the party hierarchy was Keith Joseph's revolt after the February 1974 election defeat.

Joseph never planned his excursions in advance. Even while they were under way, he was largely unaware of their significance and likely outcome. He kicked over the traces twice: first in 1969–70, and again in 1974. I was involved on both occasions as mentor, familiar, moving spirit.

Sir Keith Joseph was wealthy, good-looking and eloquent, with a first-class (though unoriginal) mind. His father, Samuel, had been Lord Mayor of London during the Second World War. He had built up a construction and property empire, Bovis, which was taken over after falling foul of a boom and bust in property-development in the early 1970s. Samuel Joseph's public service earned him the Baronetcy which Keith inherited. At Harrow and Oxford, Keith Joseph performed brilliantly. He was destined for the Bar, but the war intervened. He joined the Royal Artillery, came out as top cadet of his course, and served with relative distinction in the conflict. He was propelled by his wartime experiences into politics as a compassionate Conservative. Like many of his class, he had gained an insight from the war into the conditions of the other half, and believed that they deserved better. For him, politics was not a career but a vocation. (He married well and raised a family; his wife later divorced him because she resented being a political wife, and he remarried for love late in life).

He progressed in politics through the channels available: a seat in parliament, ministerial posts and into the cabinet as Minister for Housing, Local Government and Wales (1962-4). In government, he conformed to Conservative orthodoxies of the period: compassion expressed through the spending of the public's money on council housing, generous subsidies, high-rise tower blocks, restrictive town planning, green belts designed to look good on paper, new and expanded towns elsewhere. In the Age of Macmillan Joseph fitted in seamlessly. In opposition after 1964 he carried on balancing his business interests, constituency duties and various shadow cabinet responsibilities.

I still do not know why I was able to 'turn' him in 1969–70. He was a most unlikely rebel. We had been on mildly friendly terms since his spell in office. At the time, I wrote from London for *Haaretz*, the main Israeli newspaper. This was relevant to Keith Joseph, whose Jewish friends, and constituents in Leeds, were generally unhappy with Britain's policies in the Middle East. Since I had some grasp of the issues, and knew Hebrew and Arabic, he occasionally turned to me for guidance. Towards the end of one such meeting, as an afterthought, he showed me the draft of a speech he was planning to deliver on an economic issue, and asked for comments. I used standard journalistic techniques to knock it into shape. He was disproportionately impressed, and began to turn to me, first for sub-editing, then for editing, then for writing and finally for initiating speeches.[1]

The upshot was a series of speeches in 1969–70, in which he adopted and retailed my view that economic intervention on a 'socialist' scale by both parties had been a ghastly mistake, and that policies should take market forces more into account. His major speech on that theme was reproduced *in extenso* by *The Times*. His speeches evoked considerable attention at the time. They embarrassed the Conservative leadership, not least because their delivery coincided with a special shadow cabinet residential session convoked by Edward Heath at the Selsdon Park Hotel in Croydon to discuss the

[1] In fact, Joseph had been advised by James Douglas of the Conservative Research Department to find himself a good speechwriter; see Andrew Denham and Mark Garnett, *Keith Joseph: A Life*, Acumen, 2001, 182 [editor's note].

forthcoming general election. That meeting broke no new ground. But commentators put two and two together and interpreted Keith Joseph's excursions as the mapping of new directions in Conservative policies.[2]

Heath avoided explicitly disowning Joseph, but let it be known that the speeches were not holy writ. However, Harold Wilson picked them up, and used Joseph's arguments to raise the spectre of 'Selsdon Man' — a new brand of right-wing Tory who was hoping to destroy the policy framework of the post-war 'consensus'.[3] This further embarrassed the party leadership; it gave Labour supporters a reason to fear a Conservative victory, but also raised unrealistic hopes among Tories who wanted to believe that Heath and his colleagues harboured radical intentions. But the issue blew over, and against the odds the Conservatives won the election. Joseph was given the Department of Health and Social Security, rather than a post with more direct impact on economic policy. He promptly returned to the bosom of party orthodoxy. Our meetings slowed down to a halt. Like many Conservative ministers, he was saddled and bridled by his civil servants. They persuaded him to create a whole new tier of NHS management, creating new jobs for bureaucrats at the expense of health care. Other parts of his empire ran on as before, expanding the welfariat and its shepherds, the social

[2] See, for example, an article in *Time and Tide*, 29 January 1970, headlined 'Sir Keith — a man who talks true Tory policy' [editor's note].

[3] So potent was the myth of Selsdon Park that a group of Conservative rightwingers set up the 'Selsdon Group' to press for Joseph's policies after he had returned to office and abandoned them.

workers. All this kept him busy and out of conflict with the leadership for the duration of the Heath Government.

This is not the place to revisit in detail the various misadventures of the Conservative Party under Heath's leadership. But it is necessary to put to rest a companion myth to the fable of Selsdon Man: namely the allegation that the government performed a 'U-turn'. This idea implies that the government was set on a consciously radical course in the first place. Rather, from the outset ministers merely hoped to push through the agenda which Labour had relinquished, and to persuade the trade unions to acquiesce in a package of reforms. In return, the government would continue to regard the maintenance of full employment as its main economic priority, regardless of the real cost. Although the Industrial Relations Act (1971) was rendered unworkable by union opposition, the government still held to its own side of the bargain. But, given the choice, the union movement preferred a one-sided deal with its own creatures. Militants in the National Union of Mineworkers (NUM) precipitated a national crisis when alternative fuel supplies from the Middle East were under threat. The Conservatives called an election and went down to defeat in February 1974, hardly comprehending why the unions had spurned every well-meaning attempt at appeasement.

Under these circumstances, the Conservative leadership might have been expected to keep an open mind and take a second look at an alternative explanation for Britain's travails. But Heath did not forget or forgive Joseph's earlier flirtation with Smithian economics. When he came to set up a new shadow cabinet after his defeat in February 1974, he passed Joseph over for shadow chancellor and nominated him instead to the middle-ranking post of shadow spokesman for industry. In a fit of pique Joseph, who believed that he had earned promotion to shadow the Treasury, declined. To avoid giving the appearance of a split, it was agreed that Joseph should stay in the shadow cabinet without a specific portfolio.

Thus far it was a storm in a teacup, and probably it would have blown itself out soon enough, with Joseph eventually accepting a modest shadow post. But the idea was also floated that Joseph should establish a think tank. It was not made clear who mooted its creation, but on balance it seems likely to have been Heath, keen to keep Joseph busy and to avoid a repetition of his heretical statements in 1969–70. Since the party already had the Conservative Research Department (CRD) and the Conservative Political Centre (CPC), it was difficult to make a case for yet another similar body. But if the additional think tank was likely to do little good, it could do no harm. To stop it going astray Heath appointed Adam Ridley, Deputy Director of the CRD, to its provisional board.

Chance, the law of unintended consequences, supervened. It would take the pen of a Balzac, Stendhal or Thackeray to depict the character of Keith Joseph. Though I worked closely with him on and off for more than twenty years, I never understood him. There was a volatility of character and mood, with violent swings from optimism to utter hopelessness, from impetuosity to apathy and the feeling that nothing could succeed. This made him very difficult to read or predict.

On this occasion, Heath failed to predict Joseph's response. He came away from the meeting of the shadow cabinet excited and determined to begin his evangelism without delay. He went home to Mulberry Walk, Chelsea, rather than to either of his offices at his company, Bovis, or the Commons. This proved decisive. At both of his offices he had names, addresses and telephone numbers of prospective think-tankers. At home, he had only mine to hand. The same afternoon he telephoned to invite me over, and the die was cast.

At one of our few meetings between 1970 and 1974, I remember Joseph complaining that an article of mine in the *Daily Telegraph*, in which I excoriated new towns, had ruined his holiday. Only towards the end of the Heath Government had we resumed more constructive contact. At the time of the three-day week, with the February 1974 election approaching, he did begin to open up to me and revive his doubts about the direction the government had taken. So it was not a complete surprise to me when he asked me to become director of his new 'think tank'.[4] But had it not happened that afternoon, it could not have happened at all. There were so many alternative candidates — 'sound men', veterans of the battle against heterodoxy. He would have taken on one or two of them, and the think tank would have been still-born. With nothing new to say it could not have attracted new money; after all, the application of 'orthodox' Conservative policies had just resulted in an economic crisis, so why should anyone pay to have the same ideas restated? As it was, Joseph was

---

[4]   The term 'think tank' is an American inelegancy which now appears to be a permanent inheritance for us. It originally denoted large organisations like RAND, Brookings, Hudson and Heritage, which were capable of undertaking multi-disciplinary studies at the behest of decision-makers and other donors. More recently it has come to designate any public-policy organisation which publishes, with or without research input.

nervous at the prospect of dissent. His offer to make me director was soon withdrawn, and it was several years before I was
even offered a full-time salaried job at the think tank. That
offer originated from Number Ten, over Joseph's head.

When the think tank's foundation was officially notified in
a press release in December 1974, the seven names mentioned
did not include mine. But I was retained as a part-time helper
at £5,000 per year, with a desk in the basement of the office on
Wilfred Street, near Victoria Station in London.[5] From the
outset efforts were made to get rid of me altogether, as a mav-
erick and ideologue. They failed because none of the other
contenders were able to write the speeches that were the
life-blood of the think tank, and indeed its *raison d'etre* in
Joseph's eyes. These were typical tribulations for a 'para-
politician, a man of ideas fallen among party-politicians', as I
described myself to the *Guardian* some years later.[6]

At the time, on the advice of his friends in the long-
established free-market think tank the Institute of Economic
Affairs (IEA), Joseph appointed a treasurer, a self-made mil-
lionaire, Nigel (now Lord) Vinson. Vinson was an enthusiast,
but his enthusiasms were simple. He favoured a tabloid
approach, and, scenting Joseph's weaknesses, did his utmost
to take over the running of the think tank. He persuaded
Joseph to appoint as director Martin Wassall, a twenty-seven
year-old official from the CBI, who had impressed Vinson

---

[5]   According to the late George Urban, the Wilfred Street
       accommodation was hardly palatial for those who worked above
       ground. It had 'tiny rooms with narrow creaking steps.... Mean,
       cramped, undignified and without central heating' (Urban,
       Diplomacy and Disillusion, 162).

[6]   AS in *Guardian*, 29 June 1981.

with an article he had written in favour of profits. I gathered that in addition to Vinson's desire to run the show himself, Joseph had a thing about our mutual Jewishness; for both the chairman and director to be Jewish might seem too much, he mused. I swallowed my pride and persevered, conscious that history was still there for the making. I did persuade Joseph not to use the phrase 'Social Market' in the name of the new organisation. I disparaged this German neologism as a fad-phrase which meant everything and hence nothing. I argued successfully for a neutral-sounding name which might create its own patina over time. The title eventually chosen was the Centre for Policy Studies (CPS).

The decision to set up the think tank had been taken early in March 1974. Since it had to raise its own finance, Joseph decided that he must make some speeches which would attract attention. But what was he to say to make bruised businessmen part with their money? It stood to reason that to attract new money over and above existing contributions to Conservative causes, he must explain why things had gone so badly wrong, and how they might be put right. Joseph remembered the recognition I had brought him in 1969–70 (though not necessarily the difficulties it had brought him with the media and his colleagues). At his request I produced a speech. Most of the next three months were taken up with efforts from the Heath camp to persuade him not to make it. He hankered after something more anodyne, in order not to annoy his colleagues. Draft speeches went back and forth between us. Eventually Joseph took the plunge. We agreed on a speech to be given at Upminster, part of the outer-London suburban sprawl at the eastern extremity of the District Line in spite of its Rupert Brooke-ish name.

The text of the speech[7] was distributed by the Conservative Central Office. But there was no prior warning that this was to be anything special.[8] Even the title took the bull by the horns. 'This is no time to be mealy-mouthed: intervention is destroying us'.[9] The theme was that for the past thirty years the Conservatives had been mistaken in attempting to make the economy and society work under the burden of socialist measures. Joseph pointed out that compared with our neighbours in North West Europe we had

> the longest working hours, the lowest pay and the lowest production per head. We have the highest taxes and the lowest investment... we have tried to take short cuts to Utopia.

He drew the vital distinction between popular policies, and policies whose eventual results would be popular. Instead of improving life, the former policies had overburdened the economy:

> the private sector has been weighed down by the burden of taxation, subsidies to nationalised industries... the public sector has been draining away the wealth created by the private sector.

Politicians' speeches which have radically changed views over time can be counted on the fingers of one hand. I myself participated crucially in the Joseph–Thatcher initiative of the

---

[7] Reprinted in the Appendix, below.

[8] Joseph was rebuked for this by Harry Bourne, the *Telegraph's* magisterial political correspondent, who was annoyed that his attention had not been drawn to the speech in advance.

[9] Reprinted in the volume of Joseph's speeches entitled *Reversing the Trend*, CPS, 1975, 5-10; See Appendix.

mid-seventies, which effected radical change in Conservative leadership and policy. Yet I should be at a loss to explain why some of my initiatives succeeded in moving mountains while others fell on stony ground. Tides of opinion ebb and flow from whatever cause, and challenge politicians to react as best they can.

After all the humming and hawing, the effect of the Upminster speech was electric. Though only a minority of Conservatives — MPs included[10] — agreed with Joseph at the time, an influential minority felt that someone was speaking for them. He became almost overnight the hero of the hour. He basked in this attention. Everyone seeks approval, but his need was extreme, almost pathological. The warmth of the reception encouraged him to further boldness, embodied in a series of speeches which reiterated commonsense economics. The most memorable, delivered at Preston on 5 September, was as critical of the Conservatives' doctrines and policies as of Labour, and argued that 'inflation is caused by governments'. Joseph frontally attacked what had been the main staple of Heath's economic policy — deficit-financing, combined with wage and price controls.

Much of what then seemed revolutionary in the speech is now commonplace, and would hardly seem worth saying. At the time, it caused a furore. Sir Ian Gilmour went so far as to write to Joseph personally, arguing that under no circumstances should the party's past policies be categorized as misconstrued. Again there had been pressure to stop Joseph

---

[10] Mrs Thatcher, who did not read the text in advance, told me that she admired its 'economy of words', which was accurate as far as it went, but not its main characteristic.

speaking out, and I was unable to prevent him from showing drafts to all and sundry, resulting in numerous changes which I did my best to edit out. On more than one occasion I offered to withdraw from the whole exercise. In any case, I was not being paid at this time.

Instead of swimming with the tide Joseph had begun to change its direction. As he wrote in his first collection of speeches (published under the title of *Reversing the Trend*)

> it was only in April 1974 that I was converted to Conservatism. (I had thought that I was a Conservative but now I see that I was not really one at all).[11]

He credited me with his 'conversion'. As he wrote in a Conservative Central Office publication to celebrate the tenth anniversary of the 1979 election victory:

> From 1974, Margaret Thatcher's instincts and Alfred Sherman's economic education of me led the three of us together to establish the Centre for Policy Studies. Alfred drafted two speeches which I made at the time; they proved influential, and, of course, controversial'.[12]

In fact, Joseph's account greatly exaggerated the input of Margaret Thatcher at this early stage. After the Upminster speech had attracted some financial support, as we had hoped, Joseph told me that he intended to invite Mrs Thatcher to join as deputy chairman. I pricked up my ears. Some months previously, when asked who might succeed

---

[11]　*Reversing the Trend*, 4.

[12]　Keith Joseph, 'Stepping Stones to Power', in *The First Ten Years: A Perspective of the Conservative Era that Began in 1979*, Conservative Central Office, 1989, 18.

Edward Heath, I had ventured that in a certain conjuncture it might be Margaret Thatcher.[13] At that time, I had never met her. But I was impressed by the force of her beliefs even though her record as Education Secretary in the Heath Government had been no more impressive that Joseph's conduct at Health and Social Security. At that time, indeed, she expressed the belief that Joseph ought to bid for the party leadership, and blamed his hesitation on his troubled domestic situation. Perhaps she thought that his profile was more suited to Conservative leadership than hers. Edward Heath had assumed the purple from humble origins; but his fate meant that the gilt was wearing off the meritocratic gingerbread. Even so, she had known Joseph since before she entered parliament. Her willingness to play second fiddle persuaded me that she was no judge of character, for Keith was the antithesis of a leader. It was not to be her only lapse of judgement of people.

After the official announcement of the birth of the CPS, Margaret Thatcher attended the first couple of committee meetings and then ceased to come. By that time, the Conservatives had lost another general election, albeit narrowly, and Heath's position as leader was even more vulnerable. The CPS was increasingly regarded as the main focus for Conservative dissent. Ambition had finally come knocking for Joseph, as it does with all politicians. But his chances had been dashed by the Edgbaston affair. I call it the Edgbaston affair rather than the Edgbaston speech advisedly; it was not

[13] I voiced this opinion in a conversation with Barry Rose, a publisher who later produced many CPS pamphlets and Basil (now Lord) Feldman, a businessman who was prominent within the voluntary wing of the Conservative Party.

the speech itself which sank him, but his reaction to the subsequent attacks on it and him.

The speech, which he delivered on Saturday 19th October — nine days after the second general election of 1974 — was not at all bad. With hindsight there is very little in it which I would change. I had been re-reading *Moralise Public Life*, by the anti-fascist Italian priest Don Luigi Sturzo, and thought that its message was relevant to Britain's condition. It seemed to provide an opportunity to offset the economic liberals' utopian belief that if only restrictions on the market's operation were removed, a free society would burgeon. My argument was in the first place that a market economy is a necessary but not sufficient condition and, secondly, that for a market to flourish many other moral and social pre-requisites were essential. However important economics might be in politics, the 'Good Life' could not be measured by *per capita* GDP. The social framework appropriate to economic stability and growth could not be taken for granted.

Earlier in the year, Joseph had expressed concern at the growing number of one-parent families, of young mothers who had been divorced, deserted or never married. He had found evidence to support his views in *Poverty*, the journal of the Child Poverty Action Group (CPAG), and against my advice reproduced it verbatim in a *Daily Telegraph* article. I had argued that it was potentially damaging to raise issues for which we had no immediate remedies to suggest. Besides, I thought it a mistake to quote left-wing sources like CPAG, when there were many others available.[14] He ignored my advice, and used the quotation without ill effects at the time.

I went along with preparing a speech on the subject, building it around the central role of morality in politics. Unlike the Preston speech, which was geared in advance to a given date and venue, this project was unscheduled. In view of the controversial and sensitive nature of the topic, it needed to be taken carefully and slowly.

However, Joseph suddenly took the bit between his teeth. He intervened more than usual in that speech. *Inter alia*, against my repeated advice, he insisted on inserting his quotation from *Poverty*. It was a long speech, nearly four thousand words (taking more than half an hour to deliver), and covered considerable ground. It deserves re-publication at length, not least because of its continued misrepresentation. From time to time, I endeavoured to persuade Joseph to do this — my last attempt was very shortly before his death in 1994 — but characteristically he refused.

In keeping with my objective of differentiating Joseph's approach from that of economic liberals, for whom economics is central and the free market a value in itself, the speech stressed that the family and civilised values are the foundation on which the nation and its economy are built. But:

> they are being undermined. If we cannot restore them to health, our nation will be ruined, whatever economic policies we might try to follow. Economics is deeply shaped by values, by the attitude towards work, thrift, ethics, public

---

[14] CPAG's then Director, Frank Field, later came to accept many of Joseph's views on social deprivation [editor's note].

spirit... You will only have a healthy economy in a sound body politic....

Our objective is that the area of choice can be widened, that talented children of the poor may have the best education. Our party is older than capitalism, our area of concern is the whole of public life. Parents are being divested of their duty to provide for their family economically, for education, health, upbringing, morality, saving for old age, housing. When you take responsibility away from people, you make them irresponsible. When you break down traditional morals, the framework of behaviour, concepts of right and wrong, it is easier to subvert the social framework and replace it by a new monolithic edifice.

We were taught that crime, violence, wife-beating, child-beating were the results of poverty; abolish poverty and they would disappear.... We are in a position to test all these fine theories in the light of experience. Has any one of them stood the test? Real incomes per head have risen beyond what anyone dreamed of a generation back; so have education budgets and welfare budgets, so also have delinquency, truancy, vandalism, hooliganism, illiteracy, decline in educational standards. Some secondary schools in our cities are dominated by gangs operating protection-rackets against small children. Teenage pregnancies are rising; so are drunkenness, sexual offences and crimes of sadism. For the first time in a century and a half, since the great Tory reformer Robert Peel set up the Metropolitan Police, areas of our cities are becoming unsafe for peaceful citizens by night, and even some by day.

The overall theme of the speech — that social problems can be transmitted from one generation to the next in something like a 'cycle' — is now official doctrine even within 'New'

Labour.[15] The Blair Government's approach is also fully compatible with Joseph's claim that:

> The only real lasting help we can give to the poor is helping them to help themselves; to do the opposite, to create more dependence, is to destroy them morally while throwing an unfair burden on society.

The part which attracted attention and obloquy, leading to Joseph's decision not to contest Heath's leadership, came towards the end. Passages seized on and distorted by media, bishops and political enemies to misrepresent him had been designed precisely to indicate dilemmas which would affect would-be social reformers: 'The balance of our population, our human stock, is threatened'. Joseph then referred to the ubiquitous *Poverty* article, which showed

> that a high and rising proportion of children are being born to mothers least fitted to bring children into the world and bring them up. They are born to mothers who were first pregnant in adolescence in social classes four and five.... Some are of low intelligence, most of low educational attainment. They are unlikely to be able to give the children the stable emotional background, the consistent combination of love and firmness which are more important than riches. They are producing problem children, the future unmarried mothers, delinquents, denizens of our borstals, sub-normal educational

---

[15] The present government states that 'Social exclusion happens when people or places suffer from a series of problems such as unemployment, discrimination, poor skills, low incomes, poor housing, high crime, ill health and family breakdown. When such problems combine they can create a vicious cycle'. Joseph said the same thing, even if his language was less judicious. See www.socialexclusion.gov.uk [editor's note].

establishments, prisons, hostels for drifters. Yet these mothers, the under-twenties in many cases, single parents from classes four and five, are now producing a third of all births. A high proportion of these births are a tragedy for the mother, the child and for us.

Far from advocating an extensive programme of birth control, as the critics alleged, he left the question open, as the expression of a dilemma. 'Can we remoralise our national life, of which the economy is an integral part?' he asked. 'It is up to people like you and me.'

The speech could have done with polishing and debugging, but Keith was in a hurry to meet his self-adopted deadline. Looking over my first draft, my wife had warned me not to appear to be saying that the lower classes should have fewer children — as opposed to having children outside stable, supportive relationships — and I went over it looking for phrases which could be misunderstood. But it did not help. The London *Evening Standard*, which then published on Saturdays, decided to break the embargo on the speech (which had been imposed to postpone coverage for that evening's radio and TV and the morning's papers). The *Standard* blatantly misrepresented the speech as an attack on the working class's right to have children. It cited Joseph as having spoken against the 'lower class', using the term in inverted commas in its headlines, though in fact those precise words were not used anywhere in the speech.

It was at this point that fate took a hand. Of itself, the *Standard*'s attack would have done little harm. Five bulging sacks of mail — including a message from Lord Olivier, whose own record as a family man was somewhat mixed — reached Joseph over the next few days. At least nine out of ten were strongly supportive. But by then it was too late. When he learned of the *Standard* attack Joseph sought my advice, but I was out. I had gone to see a member of the Israeli government, who was on a visit to London. It was not an urgent appointment, but of course I had no idea that Joseph might need my advice at that time. As it was, when the media contacted him his nerve broke, and he began to apologise and backtrack. As a result, the yellow press and red bishops were on to him like a pack of wolves, accusing him of things he neither said nor implied. A Bishop Augustin Harris, Secretary of the Roman Catholic Bishops' committee on social affairs, accused Joseph of inaugurating the 'manipulative society', without making clear what he meant or on what he based the accusation. Members of the Labour government, including Joseph's successor at Health and Social Security Barbara Castle, joined the debate in the full knowledge that he would not fight back.

Of course, I had already been made aware of this lack of robustness and fighting spirit, which ruled him out as a potential leader and later made him ineffective as head of policy-making in Margaret Thatcher's shadow cabinet. I had, in fact, never discussed the leadership with him, not even implicitly. Joseph's parliamentary colleagues also knew him very well, and while appreciating his intellect did not see him as a leader. If he had survived the Edgbaston affair and put his name forward it seems certain that he would have stumbled again, sooner or later, because that was his nature. Subsequently his marriage broke up and his health deteriorated, with effects on his behaviour. But by then, the window of opportunity seized by Margaret Thatcher in January 1975 would have been lost for good.

Chapter 3

Margaret Thatcher's Inheritance

The Edgbaston affair ensured that Keith Joseph would be relegated from the role of Conservative Messiah to that of John the Baptist. The ensuing leadership election has been extensively chronicled elsewhere. Mrs Thatcher was elected without any clear idea on the part of the voters of how she intended to proceed. This stemmed from circumstances which antedated her and which she had played no part in creating. Heath's ousting has been described as a 'Peasants' Revolt'. Under the old system of choosing Conservative leaders, the 'peasants' need not even have been consulted. Under the new system, MPs — not peers or other grandees — were left in the second ballot with the choice between Mrs Thatcher, whom they scarcely knew, and William Whitelaw, who was seen as Heath by another name. Faced with the choice between the devil they knew and the devil they did not, they chose the latter. Enoch Powell, who might at one time have been a formidable contender, had resigned his seat before the February 1974 election and was therefore ineligible to stand.

Margaret Thatcher assumed the leadership of her party thirty years after VE day, and the subsequent landslide Labour victory. This turned out to be more significant than would appear on a superficial view. The economy is more than just objective reality: it is an intellectual, political and emotional construct which changes with time, experience and perspective. Britain had remained under the shadow of World War II much longer than after the First World War. The latter had been regarded at the time as an interruption of 'normality' — 'business as usual' was the recipe for post-war reconstruction. The belief that Britain could return to pre-war modes after 1918 played its part in hampering adaptation to the very different conditions of the twenties and thirties. By contrast, during and after World War II, the government, armed forces and home front alike had been suffused with the almost messianic sentiment that post-war Britain would be a brave new world in which the common people's contribution to the war effort would be rewarded and old wrongs righted. The consideration that five years of total war had impoverished Britain and left little largesse to distribute was ignored with compulsive denial, a mindset which has survived to this day.

By 1975 Britain had been self-consciously 'post-war' for three decades. Its leaders had been formed by war service for the most part. Cross-party wartime commitments to 'no going back to the bad old days' continued to set the tone. But by the mid-1970s the clichés were wearing thin.

Margaret Thatcher represented a generational shift. At school and university through the war and its heady aftermath, she came to regard the great post-war changes not as the foundations on which to build but as inherited problems to be tackled. 'Post-post-war' Britain's problems could be divided into three main categories: first, those which can be described as endogenous, the hardening of the economic arteries; second, those which resulted from the world wars and the cold war; and third, those which stemmed from efforts at social and economic reforms (eg nationalisation, economic planning, expanded state- and local government-provision of welfare).

Parliamentary democracy has an inbuilt tendency towards excessive expenditure. This may be partly psychological or ideological, but it is at least in part an effect of universal suffrage. When an increasing proportion of voters are non-producers, it becomes more blessed to receive than to give. By the nature of things, announcements of items of public expenditure are immediate, visible and popular for beneficiaries, whereas countervailing benefits in the form of reduced taxation are slow to arrive and difficult to perceive. Posterity has no electorate.

Consideration of this issue has been clouded by reliance on crude antitheses like 'left' and 'right' (or 'wet' and 'dry' in the Thatcher years). We should long since have been liberated from shibboleths inherited from the parade of the Estates on the Versailles tennis court in 1789. True, the 'left' for the most part is still captivated by the belief that the acquisition and disposal of goods and services by the beneficent state will bring prosperity and justice for all. But the growth of state expenditure in Britain actually owes little to socialists. Lloyd George and his allies played a major part in it. They, like Bismarck — who was their role model, saw statism both as an instrument for progress and an expedient for taking the wind out of socialist sails, unaware that its ultimate effect could turn out to be the exact opposite. Karl Marx, by telling contrast, had no illusions about the nature of the state as oppressor and exploiter on its own account. This is the main theme of his *Eighteenth Brumaire of Louis Bonaparte* (1852). Turn-of-the-century revisionists developed this theme; Marxist-Leninists ignored it, with disastrous results. By contrast, 'right wing' means little more than being opposed to the 'left's' wonder-cures. 'Right wingers' come in all shapes and sizes. Some would diminish the role of the state, others would expand it. Some see life through the prism of the armed services, and disdain 'commercialism'. Adam-Smithians are still in a minority.

State involvement in education, which began with elementary schooling to the age of thirteen and ended by nationalising most education at all ages, dates back to the 1860s and owed its inspiration to Prussia (in line with the belief that 'the battle of Sadowa was won by the Prussian schoolmaster'). Health and pensions, unemployment pay and housing go back to the beginning of the twentieth century, together with municipal enterprise: gas, water (including sewerage), electricity, museums and swimming baths *inter alia*. The Royal Mail's state-imposed monopoly, along with the gradual quasi-nationalisation of prisons, police and judicial services, together with the assimilation of the established church to secular officialdom all helped create an official, uniformed state system. Legislation of the last quarter of the nineteenth century gave impetus to the growth of the politicised and professionalized local government empires which coalesced with the national political parties and trade unions to spread further the networks of party fiefdoms with their attendant nepotism, jobbery, corruption and waste. Socialism built itself on this foundation, ostensibly to protect and benefit working people and the 'under-privileged', but often in practice to create new networks of privilege. 'Representing the working class' became an avenue to escape from it, into a middle-class lifestyle.

The historical context in which Thatcher gained office and operated has additional dimensions. There were many autonomous features — neither willed nor brought about by government or other formal agents of change — whose political implications were not always grasped at the time. First, despite a marked economic decline in relation to other countries, living standards had risen significantly since the beginning of the 1950s, and behaviour patterns had changed accordingly. Large numbers of people enjoyed relative affluence for the first time. Home- and car-ownership, foreign holidays, washing machines, modern kitchens, restaurant and take-away meals were now taken for granted, as was the role of government as generator and guarantor of this prosperity.

Side by side with affluence — as Alexis de Tocqueville had presciently warned a century and a half previously — residual poverty grew more obtrusive. The poor declined as a proportion of the population, though their absolute numbers remained high and even increased because of differential birth-rates, welfarisation and immigration. They stood out more, partly because their condition was no longer seen as the natural lot of the majority, but also because of the mind-set of academics and other participants in the poverty 'industry', whose ideology and temperament impel them to accentuate the negative. In politics, perceptions count at least as much as realities. The plight — real or alleged — of the poor was heavily scored in the media and in opinion-making and policy-making circles. It therefore pre-empted corresponding attention and expedients on the part of the Conservative leadership. So, paradoxically, far from solving the political problems associated with poverty, increasing affluence exacerbated them and pushed them to an unprecedented place on the agenda.

Second, in the two centuries following the Napoleonic Wars, Britain's overall population has grown at an unprecedented rate, from ten millions to its present sixty. Population growth over the period coincided with rising living standards and aspirations, which inevitably entailed substantial social costs and increased pressures on social-capital expenditure. Roads and railways, airports, docks and harbours, schools, hospitals and police facilities all grew *pari passu* with increasing welfare expenditures predicated by the welfare state. Social work, once the Cinderella of the social services, grew exponentially. Yet social dysfunction visibly grew; the public hears most often of the vast, costly social service empires through their highly-publicised failures.

The increasing costs generated by population growth, aspirations and dependency had to be borne by taxation, and some price increases caused by protection. They were not generally debited in the public mind to population increase, but to government expenditure *tout court*, which grew from 25 per cent of the national income in the early 1960s to 40 per cent in the mid-1970s.[1] But blaming population increase for

---

[1]   Charles Saatchi, who speaks for the Tories on Treasury matters in
         the House of Lords, argues that it is nearer 50 per cent today.

overall cost increases was taboo as 'Malthusian', given the Marxoid domination of social studies and the general climate of opinion. To point out the effects of immigration was 'racist'. Consideration of the economic consequences of immigration or population increase has been driven underground, but the effects were plainly experienced. The consequent increases, both absolute and relative, in state expenditure occurred as much under the Tories as under Labour. The unease and discomfort generated by the effects of population increase were experienced as a general, undefined distemper. Diehard Labour supporters ascribed them to the unfettered operation of capitalism, and Tories to various shortcomings of post-war society.

Frustrations generated among Tory supporters by the failure of successive governments to contain, let alone cut, public expenditure were intensified by dissatisfactions over social dysfunction generally. Family breakdown left large numbers of isolated individuals lacking a secure domestic framework. Moral relativism had become ensconced. There were growing illegitimacy rates, welfare motherhood on an ever-expanding scale, children and teenagers running wild, the drug culture, increased crime, low clear-up rates, etc.

This undertone of frustration reflected a general sense that the main political parties had failed, confirmed in the fact that while they had received almost 97 per cent of the vote between them at the 1950 general election, by February 1974 the proportion was down to three-quarters. Under the sway of the new intellectual climate after 1945 and the imperatives of universal suffrage, they competed in promising 'more'. They became over-committed, and thereby subject to an inevitable and increasing gulf between promise and performance. All parties relied on the state and interest groups to allot benefits, generating what the late Ferdynand Zweig dubbed 'collective acquisitiveness', updating the socialist R.H. Tawney's concept of 'the acquisitive society'.[2] Individual merit was replaced by collective 'rights', the concept of rights undergoing modification in the process, to mean duty-free claims and entitlements. The inflation of rights paralleled monetary inflation. I am reminded of Kipling's excoriation of the new-style liberal rights in his poem 'The Gods of the Copybook Headings' (1919):

> In the Carboniferous Epoch we were promised
>   abundance for all
> By robbing selected Peter to pay for collective Paul...
> And that after this is accomplished,
>   and the brave new world begins
> When all men are paid for existing,
>   and no man must pay for his sins.

Increasingly divorced from sources of fulfilment, rights became correspondingly expanded. Expansion of rights led to an inflation and debasement of rights. They included 'full' employment at acceptable remuneration irrespective of economic considerations; 'affordable' housing in desirable locations; access to higher education with no dilution of standards for an ever-increasing proportion of school leavers; personal security; generosity to single-parent families and the indigent elderly; inflation-proof (and recession-proof) pensions: prizes for everyone. The politicians had over-promised, but their opponents while lambasting their

---

[2]   Ferdynand Zweig, *The Worker in an Affluent Society*, Heinemann, 1961.

failure to fulfil their promises, shirked the duty of denouncing them as unrealistic and merely claimed that they in turn would fulfil them. The auction of promises seemed to legitimise itself, and politicians dared not question it for fear of being accused of callousness and (what was worse than being callous) losing elections.

It should be remembered that the Conservatives were essentially a party of government. To win elections was proof of virtue: to lose was the wages of sin. Policies were judged by their electoral acceptability. This distinguished the party from Labour, which was largely ideologically and policy-oriented and included factions which were even more comfortable in opposition. So in early 1975, when Mrs Thatcher audaciously seized the Conservative leadership, concern with electability weighed more heavily with her colleagues than policies to deal with Britain's distempers. Given the almost religious conviction with which neo-Keynesianism was held by most of the 'Establishment' — academics, civil servants and politicians — to question it was politically hazardous, courting accusations of 'monetarism', which then and for some time later was treated as anathema.

The essence of the neo-Keynesian position, derived partly from a misreading of Keynes and partly from politicians' natural hankering after painless panaceas, was that employment and production could be expanded by increasing demand and the money supply, while offsetting the resultant price and wage pressures through state controls. These policies had been tried on and off for over two millennia and had invariably failed. But hope springs eternal. During the dominance of neo-Keynesianism, ostensibly counter-inflationary measures, including subsidies, predictably made matters

worse. The combination of inflationary pressures with measures to restrict demand or control prices — driving with one
foot on the accelerator and the other on the brake — led to
what the media dubbed as 'stagflation' (i.e. stagnation co-
existing with inflation). It was generally recognised that
excessive government spending was the main cause of this
depressing cycle. The philosopher Epictetus argued that no-
one would sin if it were possible to achieve one's aims without sinning. Both Labour and the Conservatives wished to
avoid sinning, yet both found themselves doing so. Any
attempt to limit expenditure was sure to lead to hardships,
recession, contraction, bankruptcies and unemployment.
Living as they did from one election to the next — general,
local, European — interspersed by the demands of their
annual conferences, party leaderships felt imprisoned in the
short term.

Three decades of nationalisation had imposed crippling
burdens on the economy. This is not a question of ideology,
but of resource use. Post-war nationalisation in Britain was
adopted for motives which had nothing in common with its
ostensible justification. It was inherently irrational by any criteria. Though socialists justified nationalisation in terms of
giving the fruits of their labour to workers by hand and brain,
the nationalised industries became a parasitic burden on the
economy for the sole purpose of awarding privileged conditions of employment to selected, highly-unionised groups of
workers, without reference to their economic contribution.
They were not a form of production but of consumption, sub-
tracting from the national income instead of adding to it.

Coal was the loss-leader. In the late eighteenth century,
once the British invention of the steam engine had permitted

the deep mining of coal and its use to power machinery, British coal became the motor of the industrial revolution. Subsequently, however, richer and more accessible coal deposits elsewhere in the world, and the emergence of oil as a major alternative fuel, undermined the markets for British coal. The unions, mine-owners and successive governments were slow to adapt. After the Second World War, the nationalised Coal Board employed 700,000 mineworkers and other staff, mainly in uneconomic pits and often working under terrible unhealthy conditions, when cheaper, cleaner and safer sources of energy were available. With the arguable exception of South Wales, ample alternative sources of employment were available to miners. But the miners, as a mainstay of the union movement and its mythology, had persuaded the Attlee Government to buy up the mining industry far above its real market value and to run it for their short-term benefit. Emotional and intellectual conservatism made it impossible to question this decision, despite the high subsequent cost in terms of subsidies, relatively high energy costs, and retarded conversion to oil and natural gas. Obligations contracted to meet the costs of chronic lung diseases and other illnesses inseparable from deep mining added an overhang into the distant future. All these were not just accounting costs but real resources diverted from productive use: investment, healthcare, housing, tax-mitigation etc.

Much the same holds good for the rest of the nationalised sector. In order to preserve what was basically a nineteenth-century pattern of employment, Attlee and his successors channelled resources into out-of-date and uneconomic industries like iron and steel, shipbuilding, failing vehicle producers, railways, textiles and others. In the late 1940s the government decided that the cause of full employment would be advanced by expanding textile production, in spite of cogent warnings by the late Professor John Jewkes of Oxford University that British manufacturers would be unable to compete with the Indian sub-continent, with its much lower labour costs. But the price disadvantage was off-set by heavy protection, ensuring that consumers paid far more than they should have done for articles of mass consumption which featured heavily in the cost of living index. In spite of this costly protection, the wages and conditions provided by the textile industry failed to attract sufficient labour. Instead of allowing this anachronism to run itself down, the powers that be encouraged mass migration of labour from the Indian sub-continent. The economics of the welfare state are such that sections of the labour force with low marginal productivity saddle the economy with much higher costs than benefits. The immigrant workers and their above-average sized families created significant welfare costs, in education, health, and housing. Even the cheaper immigrant labour failed to restore the competitive position of British textiles, resulting in severe Asian unemployment and ethnic tensions, blighting once bustling northern cities.

On the eve of the Normandy landings in 1944 Ernest Bevin promised a sergeant of the Northumberland Fusiliers that there would be no return to pre-war mass unemployment. This was only seven years since prime minister Neville Chamberlain had expressly told a TUC delegation that the government can no more influence the level of unemployment than it can the weather. Yet such promises and hopes were enshrined in the (Keynesian) 1944 White Paper on employment, hedged in by prophylactic truisms and caveats, which nevertheless haunted successive governments after 1945. Edward Heath panicked at the prospect of one million unemployed, and buckled under challenge from the miners. The Conservative hierarchy drew the conclusion that macro-economic reform was more dangerous than it was worth, and that the miners must be humoured regardless of the cost.

The real lesson of the Heath years was the failure of 'tripartism' − i.e., close institutionalised collaboration between employers, unions and government. This had been the signature tune of the post-war era. But its attempt to create a harmony could not conceal its discordant elements. Government was sovereign and, at least in theory, directed from the centre, though its activities were often at cross purposes. Trade unions could speak with one voice on some issues and represent their members or perceived institutional interests, and even impose some discipline in rare cases. But, as the later 1970s showed, when they were torn between government promptings and the greed of their grass-roots members, trade union leaders invariably sided with the source of their salaries.

The private sector was even more tenuous. Its spokesmen lacked any power, and could seldom agree on anything. More deadly still, the spread of state economic power had by this time vitiated the very concept of the 'private' sector. As taxation and expenditure grew, increasing segments of the residual (nominally-) private sector came to depend on state largesse − in defence, building, civil engineering, transport, education, medicine, agriculture, etc. In other words, it tended to become an extension of the state sector by other means, and acted accordingly, pressing for more government spending in order to keep it afloat.

This state-orientation was intensified by two additional factors. First, directorships in the large firms were packed by former ministers and civil servants. During his spell as advisor to Harold Wilson and James Callaghan, Bernard (now Lord) Donoughue attempted to reform the 'revolving door syndrome' by which ministers and officials retired and walked into the very firms they had previously been dealing with on behalf of the taxpayer. He was defeated.

Second, nationalised industries were welcomed into the main employer organisation, the Confederation of British Industry (CBI) as important sources of finance. In her early years as prime minister, Margaret Thatcher had more to fear from the corporatist CBI than from the Trades Union Congress (TUC). A parallel process had been going on in both organisations. While employers who benefited from state spending began to dominate the CBI, unions whose members were paid directly by the state grew in membership and militancy while those in the market-exposed sector declined. Thus, 'tripartite' meetings of government and the representatives of employers and workers were not negotiations between three distinct organisations seeking to reconcile their interests for the national good. They were already bound together by a mutual interest in milching the taxpayer. Mrs Thatcher had to seek support more from the Association of British Chambers of Commerce, which was much more representative of the residual market-oriented segment of the private sector, and the Institute of Directors. Among the trade unions she could make semi-clandestine contacts with a few dissident leaders; but on the workers' side it was difficult to identify any truly independent 'intermediate institutions' with whom one could do business.

Trade unionism was one of the many innovations which Britain had bequeathed to the world, along with the industrial revolution, parliamentary democracy, constitutional monarchy, cricket and football. It had proved a mixed blessing. At the outset it performed an invaluable function, giving a new focus of identity and social cohesion to masses of people uprooted from the intimacies and inhibitions imposed by village life. It redressed the balance of power between labour and employers. But several features distorted it. First, into a dynamic industrial scene it introduced the innate conservatism — note the lower-case 'c' — of the British manual worker. The wide range of educational and economic opportunities afforded by Britain's economic development and relatively free society led to reverse social mobility, in the sense that the more enterprising and ambitious members of the labour force rose out of it, leaving an unleavened mass, prey to resentments. This undertone of resentment was reinforced by vulgar Marxism, with its crude pastiche of class struggle. Trade union activities became a form of reverse entrepreneurship, where militancy both gave emotional satisfaction and provided opportunities for social mobility through induction into the union and Labour Party hierarchies. In a trading society which needed dynamic change in order to adapt and survive, the unions acted as a drag on proceedings.

The combined effect of these developments was to make Britain the sick man of Europe. Every concession to the unions, designed to mollify them, had the diametrically opposite effect and incited further militancy. Extension of the state sector by means of nationalisation gave the beneficiaries economic immunity from the effects of strikes, over-manning and slack labour discipline. Softening of residual legal

restrictions encouraged the 'strike culture'. The economic
effects — days lost by strikes; bankruptcies; de-capitalisation;
loss of foreign investment — became too chronic to ignore. By
the mid-seventies, almost everyone agreed that 'something
should be done' about the unions. This feeling was strengthened by changes in the social base. The consumer classes who
patronised shopping malls and flew abroad for holidays
increasingly saw other unions as spoilers, even if they saw no
problem when demands were made on their own behalf. But
given the scrapping of Barbara Castle's proposed reforms ('In
Place of Strife'), Heath's defeat at union hands with Labour
backing, and obdurate Conservative opposition to tangling
with the unions, there was no certainty that there was sufficient political will to back up the desire for action.

Another burden on the economy which Mrs Thatcher had
to take into account after her election as party leader was Britain's membership of what was then called the European Economic Community (EEC), though its wider ambitions were
obvious to anyone who did not compulsively close their eyes
to them (or dissimulate). The benefits and dis-benefits are still
a matter of argument in both main parties. The most immediate and visible effects were the Common Agricultural Policy
(CAP) and the Common Fisheries Policy, though wider trading patterns were also affected. The first placed a heavy burden on the cost of living, which decisively affected wage-
demands and macroeconomic calculations. The second
gravely damaged the British fishing industry. Since it was the
Conservative Party which had brought Britain into the EEC
— indeed, membership was regarded as one of its very few
post-war achievements — there was little that Mrs Thatcher

could even try to do to mitigate its effects, though in office she did successfully renegotiate Britain's financial contribution.

In the mid-1970s, it became fashionable to say that Britain had become 'ungovernable'. This was not due to a lack of government; there was more government than ever. Yet the usual answer to Britain's palpable problems was 'the government must do something' — i.e., 'the government should do more'. This view was shared by the general public, which was now fully attuned to the post-war political culture. But it was also echoed by most politicians — the best from a sense of paternalism, the worse from a desire for additional patronage, and the rest out of inertia. The time was ripe for an 'animator, agent of change, and political enzyme',[3] capable of 'thinking the unthinkable'. This was the role which the Centre for Policy Studies was ready to play; and the workings of chance had given it a political leader with the courage to act on its ideas.

---

[3] This was AS's characterisation of the CPS, quoted in Thatcher, *Path to Power*, 252 [editor's note].

Chapter 4

Mrs Thatcher in Opposition, 1975–9

In 1975 Margaret Thatcher was thrown in at the deep end and expected to learn to swim. She was aware of the need to reverse the directions in which governments had been surging since the closing stages of World War II. The textbooks of history and political science (an oxymoron) had no techniques to offer. She began with a majority of the shadow cabinet diametrically opposed to her views. I advised her to scrap the shadow cabinet, which was a relatively recent innovation. As Leader of the Opposition after 1945, Winston Churchill had no shadow cabinet. He invited leading front-benchers to lunch at the Savoy every Friday to discuss the next week's business in the House. I suggested that she give a weekly lunch, and summon *ad hoc* groups of notables to discuss specific issues. She turned the proposal down, apparently because it offended her sense of constitutional propriety. I regretted that I had never persuaded her to read Machiavelli. True, the absence of a shadow cabinet would not have absolved her from the need to put her case in one forum or another, to reason with other viewpoints and sometimes to give priority to smooth relations over logic. But it would have eased her task.

I also suggested that she should exercise the leader's prerogative and purge the Conservative Research Department of Christopher Patten and many of his colleagues. They were actively working to undermine her (with Whitelaw's blessing), working instead on behalf of James Prior, who had run unsuccessfully in the 1975 leadership contest. Patten used his influence over policy study groups to exclude or restrain radical thinking. Among other manoeuvres, Patten leaked the details of bolder study-group proposals to the press, in order to frighten off party 'moderates' who suffered from a low panic threshold. Michael Portillo, then a CRD man in all things, was actively engaged in Patten's anti-Thatcherism before his subsequent evolutions, first to enthusiastic ultra-Thatcherism, then to 'inclusivity' and, finally, internal opposition under William Hague and Iain Duncan Smith.

Rightly or wrongly Mrs Thatcher declined to grasp that particular nettle, which continued to sting her even after she became prime minister. She had realised that she had few friends and many enemies, and seemed to take it in her stride. She learned early on that nothing she could do would change their minds, and that their dependence on her to win elections was the only thing that would keep them in line.

In opposition she endeavoured to offset the anti-Thatcherite predominance in the shadow cabinet and Central Office, through a series of speeches designed to wean the public away from naïve 'post-war reconstruction' to longer-term sustainable non-doctrinaire compassionate Conservatism. In her 1977 Iain Macleod memorial lecture she said that:

> We have learned much from the over-optimism of the imme-diate post-war era when we thought governments could do it all. We need healthy scepticism but not pessimism. We are not bound to an irrevocable decline. We see nothing as inevi-table. Men can still shape history…
>
> Because we see that welfare can be abused, we do not neglect our responsibility to help people back onto their feet and to look after the handicapped'.[1]

Here was the balance that suffused her speeches, but which the media and politicians of all parties chose to ignore or underplay. Politicians are dependent on the media as never before. In Gladstone's time, his speeches would be repro-duced *verbatim* in the next morning's newspapers, and widely read. People could then make up their own minds. Nowadays, even the most senior politicians are presented to the public by the media, rather than being able to reach them directly. Mrs Thatcher was presented as shrill and unfeeling, whereas I found her warm and an attentive listener. I once had occasion to review a book about her by the *Guardian* jour-nalist, the late Hugo Young.[2] It was strong on condemnation but weak on quotation; the reader is hard put to find out what she thought and said, but learns a great deal about what Hugo Young thought about her.

---

[1] Reprinted in Margaret Thatcher, *Let Our Children Grow Tall: Selected Speeches 1975-1977*, Centre for Policy Studies, 1977, 103-13.

[2] *One of Us: A biography of Margaret Thatcher*, Macmillan, 1989.

It is particularly important to return to the sources and ascertain what Mrs Thatcher really preached, since an increasing proportion of today's public came of age after her time in office and therefore rely on what is written about her at second hand. Far from preaching a crude ahistorical materialism, as some propaganda-disguised-as-history now presents her, she emphasised duties: the duty to be self-sufficient and also generous, to look after oneself and family but also to contribute to the wider good. In her Macleod lecture she quoted the socialist Archbishop Temple's insistence that the quest for national and Christian purpose must not be at the expense of the legitimacy of self- and family interest.[3] She argued that leaving too many duties to the state ensured that they would be neglected, and that philosophy has an essential role. It was a call for balance, not selfishness: to balance individual or family interests with wider duties, and to restore a sense of nationhood and purpose. The speech reflected the argument I was pressing on her, that the socialists had dragged economics into the centre of political discourse, while Conservatives should be setting criteria for the Good Life.

During her first two years as Leader of the Opposition, Mrs Thatcher made over a dozen set speeches outlining her philosophy and policy prescriptions. We worked on these speeches day and night, particularly of an evening and weekend at her home in Flood Street, Chelsea. Besides me, there was Ronald Miller (the actor and playwright), her PPSs John

---

[3]   For Temple (1881–1944), see Mark Garnett and Richard Weight, *Modern British History: The Essential A-Z Guide*, Pimlico, 2004, 473-4.

Stanley and Adam Butler, and her advisor John Hoskyns, a former regular soldier who had set up his own computer business, built it up, and then sold it in order to dedicate himself to public affairs. There was a meeting of minds; every phrase, every word had to earn her approval (in contrast to Keith Joseph, who often accepted and delivered speeches after a cursory reading). In addition, she fed us, sometimes preparing the food in the kitchen while talking to us seated around the dining room table.

The housewife and party leader co-existed in her. I remember arranging her first meeting with Hoskyns, Terry Price and Norman Strauss, whom I had encountered and recruited to the CPS. They spent several hours with her in Flood Street on the Saturday and Sunday. She later complained that most of their ideas, based on systems analysis, had been above her head and seemed irrelevant for immediate practical purposes. She had fed them, and now complained that they had eaten all her food and left her no usable ideas in return. I countered by offering to bring sandwiches next time I came. We laughed; John, Terry and Norman were reprieved. Later I persuaded Mrs Thatcher to retain Harold Wilson's Downing Street Policy Unit, and to put John in charge. Norman Strauss was appointed to work with him.

The CPS continued to hold lunches, dinners, seminars. People came because of the sense that it provided a line of communication with 'Her'. Some submitted papers. Once a year we held an annual conference which she addressed. But insofar as she made headway with bringing her ideas to party members and opinion-formers it was through the set speeches, and to a lesser extent thanks to Keith Joseph's missionary activities in the universities, where the rougher the ride he was given the more positive the publicity. But the problem remained that the machinery of party and government under-provides facilities for the leadership to lay its views (as opposed to sound-bites) before the nation. The Conservative Party has yet to evolve a mechanism for elaborating and updating political ideas, strategies and policies, linking public with leaders.

The gradual transformation of Mrs Thatcher from an untried party leader into a prime minister-in-waiting was complex. The first eighteen years of her life in Puritan England shaped her for ever. For her, God was a real presence. Duty was paramount. Much of her life was taken up with implicit or explicit protest against the decline of traditional values, which characterised the second half of the twentieth century. In part I might have helped her to recognise the significance of Grantham, but much of Grantham was embodied in her, waiting to emerge. Her typical style became more robust and argumentative, with a more homely form of address than Conservative politicians had affected, metaphors and similes drawn from everyday life. She spoke to and for women on the council estates who aspired to something better. But comfort had to be earned, and prosperity should never be flaunted. Her belief that people should not live up to their income — let alone above it — was demonstrated by her own modest lifestyle.

During those four-and-a-half years I often felt that the shadow cabinet and Conservative Central Office were like the Tower of Babel; we spoke different and mutually incomprehensible languages. Leading members of the shadow cabinet were not so much colleagues as plenipotentiaries, less concerned with opposing the Labour government than in internal manoeuvres, and clipping Mrs Thatcher's wings. In those years they found it easier to attack Keith Joseph than to turn their fire on the real target. Two important speeches made by Joseph soon after Mrs Thatcher's leadership victory were subjected to deliberate distortion: his Stockton Lecture, 'Monetarism is Not Enough,'[4] and his speech to the 1975 Conservative Party conference. The first explained that the government's IMF-induced policy of squeezing the money supply would damage the wealth-creating sector unless it was accompanied by meaningful cuts in public expenditure; the second explained that Conservatives should not seek the 'middle ground' between capitalism and socialism, but rather to find 'common ground' with the British people. He argued that accommodation to socialist measures in the name of the will-o'-the-wisp of the 'middle ground' had created a 'ratchet effect', and every Labour initiative had pushed the middle ground leftwards. These were both constructive contributions to political debate, but Joseph's critics felt that they had answered him by giving him the nickname of the 'Mad Monk'. I began to be mentioned in press attacks inspired by Mrs Thatcher's opponents, appearing as a 'guru', 'Svengali' or 'Rasputin' (obviously there was room for more than one mad monk in Mrs Thatcher's entourage).

Joint shadow cabinet publications, like *The Right Approach* (1976) and *The Right Approach to the Economy* (1977) were not coherent sequential statements of cause and effect, strategy and tactics, but rather strings of homilies which were chosen because they would not provoke trouble among Mrs Thatcher's colleagues. I was excluded from participating in

---

[4] Published as a CPS pamphlet in 1976.

the production of *The Right Approach to the Economy*. Fear of 'ideology' — one of the new deadly sins — was translated into a phobia against ideas of any kind.[5] This resulted in the loss of several years which could have given the party what the French called 'the cure of opposition'. Instead of preparing for government under new circumstances with renewed philosophy, strategies and policies, and castigating the socialist government, the Conservatives looked like a party without direction.

In one sense, Conservatism is doomed to be in permanent crisis, always a step behind change, seeking to come to terms with what it had opposed, or at least decried and tried to preclude. But this is precisely what gives it its representative character, because most people are generally one step behind change. While socialists are trapped in a doctrine which is treated like holy writ, Conservatives can afford to explore the workings of fate and chance. What hobbled British Conservatism in the sixties and seventies was not their Conservatism but their entrapment in Butlerite dogma, excesses of state control, prices and incomes policies, job conservation — socialism by another name. Escaping from this entrapment ate up years of early Thatcher leadership which could have been better spent. Certain themes were off limits. Family breakdown and growth in the numbers of single mothers, continued high levels of immigration, the qualities of people in the lower reaches of society remained taboo, although Mrs Thatcher had strong views on those subjects. That was her

[5]   My riposte to those who used against me the sinister French word *ideologue* has been to cite Socrates's telling condemnation, uttered during the last tragic hours of his life (and recorded in the *Phaedo*) of 'misologue', hater of reason.

judgement; as a political amateur I was not really qualified to question it.

In that sense, time in opposition partook of the nature of purgatory. She could only fight to survive till she became prime minister. She was under continuous attack — open and veiled, direct and indirect — from inside the party no less than outside, where she was subjected to sniping from the government and the media. She had decided at the outset not to riposte. I remember only one occasion when Heath's behaviour had particularly annoyed her. The two of us were alone at the time, and she exclaimed in a quiet but firm voice: 'The bastard, the bastard, the bastard!'. That was that. It was as though since she could trust no-one, there was no point in making a bigger issue of it; one simply had to get on with the job. I was reminded of the saying: 'uneasy lies the head that wears a crown'.

She spent much of the time on the road, keen to meet as many party members and voters in person as possible. Great occasions when she spoke to a mass audience, and could hope for TV coverage, were few. At the annual party conference, the leader's speech on the Friday afternoon constituted the climax of a week of meetings, functions, lunches, dinners and cocktail parties where the Tory faithful meet only other Conservatives. The leader's address on the Friday afternoon should constitute the climax of a week of togetherness. The audience in the hall provided a sounding-board for a speech which also had to be projected to the nation and the world. Preparation for this absorbed enormous nervous energy. During the daytime and evenings, when she did her rounds, she was all patience, sweetness and light. In the late evening, when our writers' conclave met, her nerves would be taut.

She seemed worried that the speech would fall flat, that she would lose her audience, though there was not the slightest danger that this might happen. Indeed, during her last leader's speech, just a few weeks before she narrowly failed to beat Michael Heseltine by enough votes to secure re-election, her reception by the conference had been as enthusiastic as ever. But the party faithful were one thing; the MPs were quite another.

The leader's speech partook of the nature of a religious occasion. The relationship between the speaker and the audience was sometimes magical. At the time, we fought over every word. Meanwhile, Patten and Adam Ridley of the CRD fought to keep the speech as far as possible within pre-Thatcherite parameters. John Hoskyns and I battled to make it as Thatcherite as possible, generally supported by David (now Lord) Wolfson, her Chief of Staff. Ronald Miller was more interested in style and humour, while the Principal Private Secretary would be more concerned with propriety. We proposed, she disposed. She also emphasised the need for what she called 'clap lines'. Audience participation through clapping is part of the process. How far our doctrinal disputes impinged on the audience or the media would be difficult to say without much research. The media usually had their minds made up anyway.

During the period of opposition it was far from certain how the Tories would fare at the forthcoming general election. Had James Callaghan gone to the country in Autumn 1978, as widely expected, there is every reason to suppose that he might have won. Political history would have been very different. Margaret Thatcher would have been replaced as Conservative leader, Labour would not have split, Denis Healey would have succeeded as prime minister in due course, and the Conservative crisis would have come much sooner. We still have no clear idea why Callaghan decided not to run. Mrs Thatcher's closest supporters had all been briefed to expect him to use the occasion of the TUC conference to announce the election. It made sense. He ran a minority government; the Conservative opposition was clearly divided, and had not been very successful facing an experienced prime minister. But instead of seizing his opportunity Callaghan told the TUC that the election would be delayed, with a music hall song and a little jig. True, he could not know at the time that the strikes of 'the winter of discontent' would occur and that he would lose the Commons vote (28 March 1979) on Scottish devolution,[6] thus ensuring that he began a general election campaign on the back foot. But both eventualities — union unrest and conflict over devolution — were not impossible to foresee. His decision to postpone the election deserves more note, as a major turning-point in contemporary history.[7]

---

[6]   Ironically, although the frustration of nationalist parties at Labour's botched devolution project helped propel the Conservatives back into power, my efforts to interest Mrs Thatcher in the subject met a brick wall. She knew nothing about Scotland and was totally out of sympathy with Scottish national feeling. The Conservative party paid (and is still paying) a heavy price for this.

[7]   While this subject continues to be debated, Labour's private polls did not convince Callaghan that his party could win an overall majority in Autumn 1978; and he was understandably tired of minority government. See Kenneth O. Morgan, *Callaghan: A Life,* Oxford University Press, 1997, 626-50 [editor's note].

In the event, the last months of Conservative opposition were spent under the shadow of forthcoming elections, and generated even stronger pressures than usual for the leadership to say nothing which might conceivably give a handle to Labour. This came to mean saying as little as possible about anything. Though the advertisement-led, package-politics was a cloud no larger than a man's hand in the late 1970s, I had serious misgivings about the style of our opposition propaganda. Dependence on advertisers and public-relations advisers was taking root. I questioned this, arguing that winning support for policies needed quintessentially different approaches from the selling of soap-powder. For example, the slogan 'Labour isn't working', which featured on a poster in the year before the election, ignored the consideration that the economic recession imposed by Healey at the behest of the International Monetary Fund (IMF) would intensify during the next year or two, thereby increasing unemployment whatever an incoming government might do. As things turned out, the economic policies of the Thatcher Government made unemployment worse than it might otherwise have been by continuing Labour's squeeze on the private sector. More generally, I was concerned that when these wealthy advertising agencies worked nominally for lower-paid party officials, unhealthy tensions could develop.[8]

During the 1979 general election campaign I ran a speech-writing room for Mrs Thatcher. After the victory she sent me a note of thanks:

---

[8]   AS in *Guardian*, 20 July 1987.

We are over the first hurdle; now for the real battle. In that I hope you will play as important a part as you have done over the past few years. You have been a constant inspiration to Keith and myself through difficult times. Your creative mind has been responsible for many skirmishing victories in the great battle of ideas, which I am convinced we are on the way to winning. But to be sure of doing so we will need you on hand at all times.[9]

The 'first hurdle' had been difficult enough to surmount, but the 'real battle' had been lost before it began. The rethink of politics, economics, taxation, subsidies, nationalised industries, religion, national identity, immigration and the changing face of British society which we had advocated at the CPS was postponed *sine die*. As a result, Mrs Thatcher inherited the premiership in 1979 together with the policies set by her predecessors, and without the intellectual or administrative framework for reshaping them. She had to wrestle with them simultaneously with problems of the day — prices, currency, public-sector union militancy, Soviet re-assertiveness, a civil service set in its ways. During the next ten years she was to innovate boldly and successfully in trade union reform, privatisation, and elsewhere. But these achievements came later than they need to have done, while other much-needed reforms (eg local government finance, the place of sterling in wider economic policy, civil service hypertrophy) were not tackled in time. These failures can be

[9]   Letter from MT to AS, 5 May 1979, in possession of the author. Parts of this letter are reprinted in Richard Cockett, *Thinking the Unthinkable: Think-Tanks and the Economic Counter-Revolution 1931-1983*, HarperCollins, 1994, 265, though the author mistakenly dates it 11 May [editor's note].

attributed to the unsatisfactory record of the Conservatives in opposition.

Chapter 5

The First Thatcher Government, 1979–83

I remember a conversation with Lord Donoughue — then founding-head of the Downing Street Policy Unit and an acute observer of the government machine — not long before the 1979 general election. He warned me that within weeks of Thatcher taking over, the civil service would present proposals which would tie her hands for years to come. He might have added that the civil servants would act through her cabinet colleagues and other branches of the Establishment.

Our current social and political theory is woefully weak on the civil service and other segments of the Establishment. The civil service is not politically neutral, colourless and tasteless as textbooks suggest. It is an estate of the realm, with its own world-view, interests and priorities. I am indebted to an essay by the late Professor Sam Finer, questioning the almost

universal approval of the nineteenth-century Northcote-
Trevelyan reforms, which created a professional civil service
appointed through competitive examinations. As Finer
argues, this created a caste insulated from the values and concerns of professional and business communities, generating
its own endogenous criteria and *modus operandi*. Its interests
largely coincide with those of the growing state apparatus. In
Karl Marx's phrase, its circumstances have shaped its consciousness. For one thing, the untidiness and unpredictability of the market evoke disfavour when compared to the
logical, predictable and controllable operations of government. Every department wishes to protect itself against loss
of functions and personnel; the laws of corporate survival
operate. Labour in office is expansionist, which the civil service likes, even though 'Bennite' exuberance can cause concern. Conservative ministers are traditionally passive, and
leave their civil servants to run the show. They might rail
against bureaucracy in their speeches, but they can be relied
upon to do nothing about it.

The fate of Keith Joseph is instructive here, for all his personal idiosyncrasies. His tendency to wilt under pressure
remained after the Edgbaston affair, contrasting oddly with
his courageous speeches to hostile university audiences during the opposition years. He was upset by the continued war
between the CRD and the CPS. The conflict raised the question of the CPS's identity, *raison d'etre*, role and function. But
Joseph was reluctant to discuss these issues comprehensively
or even casuistically. He tried to keep the CPS as far as possible from the Conservative policy-making and presentational
system, in order to minimise friction with the CRD. There
were days when he deliberately spent hours walking

between the CPS at Wilfred Street, his own room at the Commons, and his office at Bovis, in order to avoid arguments about or between Patten and myself. In his peregrinations between offices, Joseph carried a briefcase bulging with books. The weighty volumes that fed his boundless intellectual curiosity injured his neck, and made him ill.

Prior and Patten's campaigns against me, really directed against Mrs Thatcher, increasingly disorientated him. Sometimes he fought back, but often he blamed me for antagonising his opponents, without ever specifying what precisely he objected to. He would ask me to draft articles, speeches and book reviews, then take fright because they might provoke objections from colleagues or people in his constituency — mainly, it seemed, left-leaning clergymen. He would question me intensely and minutely on them, then declare that he was too busy to proceed with them, although they were his initiatives in the first place. I remember one morning, when I was working at home in Kensington, he turned up unannounced by taxi, with the leader page article which he had torn out from the *Financial Times*. He thrust it at me, urged me to read it, and vanished. I read it — typical journalistic wordiness, with no new ideas — came to the office, and asked him what he wanted me to do. He was surprised, and said that he had just wanted me to read it.

In 1978 the incumbent of the marginal Ilford North seat, with a relatively high proportion of Jewish voters, died. During the by-election campaign efforts were made to enlist Jewish sympathies with unrestricted Commonwealth immigration. I encouraged Joseph to go down with a speech pointing out that Britain was a small over-crowded island, with limited capacity to absorb. Hence, Jewish voters should share the concerns of their Gentile fellow-citizens on this matter. He came under fire for his speech, from the Left, including 'professional Jews' who claimed to be the authentic spokesmen of their co-religionists, from the *Daily Express* and even from the *Times*. He began to panic and 'wobble' — to use Mrs Thatcher's word — but I was on hand to rally him. He stood his ground and his boldness paid off. The Conservatives won the seat, and according to an ITN poll the swing among Jews was twice that of Gentiles.[1]

The strike at 'Fort Grunwick', a photograph processing plant at Willesden, North London, was another example. The powerful Transport and General Workers Union (TGWU), keen to expand into new fields, had decided to organise the workers in photograph processing and allied trades into the union, much against their will.[2] They persuaded the leaders of the clerical workers' union, APEX, to join them in this endeavour, which entailed calling strikes over the heads of employees, and intimidating them into joining. The general secretary of APEX, Roy Grantham, later confessed that he had made an error in supporting this enterprise. But at the time, Labour leaders rallied to their support: Shirley Williams and Fred Mulley demonstratively joined the picket lines.[3] The mass rallies and intimidation directed mainly against Asian women workers in saris were covered by TV,

---

[1] The defeated Labour candidate was Tessa Jowell, later a cabinet minister [editor's note].

[2] For a vivid contemporary account of this significant incident, see Joe Rogally, *Grunwick*, Penguin, 1977.

[3] Williams and Mulley were both sponsored by APEX (as was the Chancellor, Denis Healey). While not excusing their actions, this

but the Conservatives did not react. Worse still, at an annual CBI conference a leading member denounced Grunwick for allegedly resisting 'free' trade unionism.

I persuaded Keith Joseph to take a hand. In a speech released to the media, he explained how the strike was not an expression of the workers' will but on the contrary an attempt to impose on them the will of the professional politicised union bureaucracy. I believed that much more was at stake than the fortunes of a single factory. The speech challenged Shirley Williams and other Labour moderates to reconsider the company they were getting into. In his peroration, Joseph said:

> We were always told — the Marxists and the thugs are a minority; there is another Labour movement which should be our natural ally. Let us join them on the middle ground. I wish this were true. But where are they? Will the real democratic socialists please stand up? Will they denounce the rentamob siege of Grunwick? Will they denounce fraternal party links with the concentration-camp regimes of Eastern Europe? Will they speak and act for the rule of law? Will they recognise that no democracy is worthy of the name without the right not to join a union, and indeed that no union can be truly democratic when membership is compulsory?
>
> The Battle of Grunwick sorts out the democrats on the one hand from the red fascists and time-servers on the other. The

---

certainly provides some of the background to the dilemma which faced them at that time [editor's note].

Labour democrats have yet to stand up and be counted. Do they exist? I still hope so, but seeing is believing.[4]

Joseph was fiercely criticised for his intervention. Strictly speaking, these matters were the responsibility of James Prior, as front-bench spokesman on Employment. But his speech had immediate effects — in the media, in parliament, and on public opinion. Grunwick was saved, the strike collapsed, Shirley Williams back-pedalled, and the feeling that 'something could be done' about the unions gained momentum. It looked as if Joseph was far from being a spent force. But it was not until shortly before his death in December 1994 that Labour's Employment spokesman Tony Blair accepted Tory reforms which outlawed the union 'closed shop'. It was typical of Keith that, despite his partisan attachment to the Conservative Party, he freely acknowledged that Labour's democrats had 'stood up to be counted' at last.

After the election victory in 1979 Joseph resigned as Chairman of the CPS on the grounds that he should not solicit subscriptions from businessmen whom he would be facing across the table in his new capacity of Secretary of State for Industry. Probably his decision made little difference to his subsequent performance, which was little short of disastrous. The Keith Joseph of his previous ministerial experiences returned; civil servants led him by the nose. He assumed the air of a haunted man, like a rabbit caught in a car's headlights. He continued to shore up the costly, failing nationalised British Leyland (BL) company at the urging of his officials who

---

[4]   Keith Joseph, speech at Doncaster Racecourse Restaurant, 24 June 1977 (Conservative Central Office handout).

wished to preserve their empire intact. His strictures during opposition were forgotten. The civil servants' argument that suppliers would suffer if BL was closed down was demonstrably fallacious. For one thing, many supplies were generic, not specific to any particular marque, so fewer BL cars and trucks purchased would mean more demand for others to be kitted out in the UK. Second, only the least efficient manufacturers depended on BL's custom. Third, wages and conditions in BL, maintained by subsidies, had a deleterious effect on wage demands and work- discipline throughout industry. But, as I complained in a publication at the time, one lame duck brings more joy in Whitehall than ninety-nine healthy firms. Joseph continued to prop up Tony Benn's creation, mainly by obliging nationalised bus companies, the armed services and company fleets which required tax privileges, to buy its products and thereby to shield the shop-stewardised labour force from the effects of its own malfeasance.

Worse still, Joseph reneged on the party's specific promise to restore the shipyards — which had been nationalised by Callaghan as a favour to the unions but never paid for — to their owners. The civil servants fed him the argument, which he swallowed and retailed to me, that if the Conservative government fulfilled its promise to restore the yards to their owners, those shareholders who had despaired and sold their shares would be worse off than those who had held onto them. Therefore, to return the yards to their owners would discriminate against those shareholders who had sold up. That he could accept such an argument suggested that he was gripped by a psychosis immune to reason. At the time, I cited the apocryphal case of the Aberdeen council bus service which had decided to cut the cross-town fare from sixpence to four pence, thereby provoking mass protest from the many Aberdonians who undertook the journey on foot to save money and suddenly found their daily saving cut from a shilling to eight pence. My argument was to no avail. Nationalisation of the shipyards, against which the Conservative Party had fought hard in opposition, was duly completed. A huge costly superstructure was set up, billions were poured in, and after a few years shipbuilding in Britain, which at the beginning of the century produced most of the world's shipping, came to an end.

Margaret Thatcher then moved Joseph to the Department of Education, where it was hoped he might introduce reforms. But once again he was no match for the civil servants and the educational establishment. They persuaded him to replace O Levels with the GCSE, which diluted standards. I remember his fraught behaviour when he attended a session of the CPS Education Committee, which was beginning to show a critical face. Since he appeared to resent any reference to ideas which were once common ground between us, I remained silent. He suddenly shouted at me, asking why I was hiding my thoughts from him. It was quite embarrassing; he was obviously torn by tensions between his old, better CPS self and the new pressures he was facing from officials and educationalists. In 1986 Mrs Thatcher came to the conclusion that he was a liability, and felt obliged to send him to the backbenches and thence to the House of Lords.[5]

[5] There was, however, talk at the time that in her desperation to keep Joseph in the cabinet Mrs Thatcher hoped to give him a post without portfolio, but that he opted for retirement instead; Denham and Garnett, *Joseph*, 404-5 [editor's note].

Keith Joseph's rapid reversion to type was the more damaging because Mrs Thatcher needed staunch allies as much as ever after her 1979 election victory. Her first cabinet reflected the balance of opinion in the higher reaches of the Conservative Party — i.e., the majority were determined opponents who still hoped that she would fail and be replaced by one of their own. Mrs Thatcher herself was not a good administrator, in the sense of devising strategies and ensuring that they were followed. She tended to act as though speeches and declarations sufficed.

In the early days I had made two proposals which I thought essential if she were to convert her rhetoric into action. I advised her to establish a 'territorial army' of advisors who would shadow politicians and senior civil servants while in opposition and prepare to be recruited as full-time temporary civil servants when the Conservatives regained power. I also argued for the creation of a separate prime minister's department, with its own ministers and (carefully selected) civil servants who would stay there through their whole careers. The proposal was tried out on party grandees, who predictably turned it down. 'Civil servants are honourable men', they argued. My Shakespearean quip — 'so are they all, all honourable men' — did not go down well. Later I recommended on several occasions, in discussions and memoranda, that she should reshape her governing structures to the imperatives of big 'joined-up' government. Once again her penchant for 'propriety' ruled against my advice.[6]

Modern cabinets are dominated by spending departments. Though according to hallowed theory they should compete among themselves for scarce resources, leaving the prime minister and the chancellor to hold the ring, in practice the spending ministers, under the influence of their departments, tend to combine to press for more government expenditure. The centre has rarely been capable of resisting. Hence government spending has grown both absolutely and relatively, *hinc illae lacrimae*. Tony Blair was one of the very few premiers in a strong enough position to resist this tendency during his first administration, partly because of his massive electoral victory and the collapse of the Tory vote, and partly thanks to his deal with the Chancellor, Gordon Brown. Margaret Thatcher began in a weak position *ab initio* thanks to the circumstances of her rise to the Conservative leadership. Despite all the rhetoric she never managed to control the spending departments.

The Thatcher Government began with a dramatic economic reform — the abolition of exchange controls. But the Treasury team — headed by Geoffrey Howe, with his Permanent Under-Secretary Sir Douglas Wass (later Lord Croham) and guided by Adam Ridley from the CRD — perpetuated the post-IMF policies of Denis Healey. So the private sector, particularly manufacturing, was squeezed in order to keep the miners, iron and steel workers, strike-happy BL *et al* in the

---

[6]   In this respect Tony Blair has been more radical than Thatcher; but then his treatment of the House of Lords suggests that a dose of constitutional 'propriety' is no bad thing [editor's note].

style to which they had become accustomed. Majority opinion in the cabinet favoured this approach, partly from fear of antagonising the unions and other vested interests, and partly because politicians tend to carry on in a straight line unless *force majeure* obliges them to change tack. This, it might be said, is human nature; but it is human nature under specific conditions. In a free market a firm can be forced to revise policies by messages from the profit and loss account; management will only fail to respond at a cost to themselves and their employees. But politicians have no such automatic feedback loops. They need to think and re-think, to learn from experience. But vanity and self-importance diminish their readiness to admit to error, even implicitly. Hence politics generally lags behind life.

Once in office the Conservatives were confronted with the Clegg recommendations for substantial pay increases to civil servants and other public-sector employees. It was decided that this gambit by the outgoing government should be honoured. Inflationary pressures were reinforced by demands from the nationalised industries: coal, iron and steel and Keith Joseph's BL, among others. This induced yet more inflation, which in turn spurred government on to drastic new squeezes, through high interest rates. Since the public sector is generally more highly-capitalised per worker, in terms of both fixed and working capital, each job 'saved' in the public sector through subsidies and feather-bedding cost several in the private, wealth-creating sector. Moreover, as I demonstrated at the turn of 1981–2, the monetary squeeze had forced up the value of the pound sterling, to the detriment of industrial exports and British industry's competitive ability in the domestic market. The squeeze was thereby self-perpetuating, and self-reinforcing.

The CPS did what it could to help. At the time, 1979 and early 1980 seemed like a golden age. Mrs Thatcher had not accepted my idea of a 'territorial army' of advisers, but I was not alone: John Hoskyns and Norman Strauss were in positions of influence. I was awarded a full-time salary (the equivalent of that of an under-secretary of state but without the non-contributory pension allowance) and moved out of the Wilfred Street basement to a room with natural light. Relations with the CRD seemed to be normalised. My working relationships with Richard Ryder, who was translated from Mrs Thatcher's personal assistant to political secretary, and with her newly-appointed PPS, Ian Gow, were excellent.

We had been prevented by Keith Joseph from running policy groups in the opposition years, as they would have seemed to be running in competition with the 'official' party groups serviced by the CRD. This ban was lifted just before the 1979 victory — though too late to influence the manifesto — and several groups were established across a wide range of key subjects. The Health Group was broadly-based, with medical men, insurance specialists, operational researchers and economists. In 1980 it submitted a proposal for a pilot study into costs and performance in the NHS. Our argument was that since the NHS is based on budgetary control, the performance-counterpart of every penny spent must be measured in order to make informed allocation of resources. Money spent on buildings, on staff and equipment, costs and benefits of operations, etc, all need balancing. Our group therefore proposed a four-year study, costing £800,000, to be carried out by the Management Sciences Department of the

Imperial College of Science, Technology and Medicine, whose head, Professor Samuel Eilon, was a member of the group.

Our proposal's fate epitomised the problems facing outsiders in their dealings with office-holders. Our views and proposals were usually submitted to civil servants, whose comments were treated as official secrets, which could not be relayed back to us except in the most general terms. Almost inevitably the answer was 'no go', and we had no opportunity to answer their detailed criticisms. This nullified our effectiveness in most cases, leaving the field to the civil servants. In the case of the proposal for a pilot study on health, we gained the following picture of the objections. First, it would cost too much. Second, four years would be much too long (it would have been completed by 1985, whereas three years later a select committee chairman was able to argue that lack of data on the NHS precluded reorganisation). Third (the argument went) they already knew everything they needed to run the NHS. Fourth, nothing we could adduce would be of help to them. Finally, they were thinking of doing a study along the same lines anyway, and were better fitted to do this inside the Department. That was par for the course. The proposal fell by the wayside.

Our education study group produced copious material. In the early days, it seemed that we might change the shape of things. The group's chairman, Caroline Cox, was elevated to the House of Lords. The education establishment, which had brought standards steadily down, and fought off Callaghan's serious bid for reform in 1976, thwarted all Lady Cox's efforts. Standards continued to fall, although Joseph made some brave efforts before lapsing into passivity in the face of officialdom.

Education, and higher education in particular, is a stark illustration of the limitations of 'Thatcherite' reform. She inherited a problem which went back to the fifties, when Harold Macmillan was unwise enough to set up a Committee on Higher Education. Its chairman, Lord Robbins, was nominally a free market economist who argued against bloated state expenditure. With the help of some Marxoid dons he decided that higher education deserved more lavish treatment. The intellectual quality of the Robbins report (1963) may be judged by its thesis that the success of the Soviet economy could be explained primarily by the number of graduates, at a time when Soviet economic failure was manifest to all but true believers. The report urged that everyone capable of 'benefiting' from a university education — a concept capable of many definitions, but never clearly defined — should be given one at the expense of the taxpayer.

For centuries England managed with three universities, while Scotland, with a tenth of the population, had the same number. The impulse that led to successive waves of university expansion beyond that required to accommodate population growth owes more to egalitarianism than to proven economic need. Thus the idea that different people have differing intellectual potential — which had been taken for granted since the dawn of time — has not been refuted but simply made into a taboo. The same impulse rules out any recognition that numerical expansion devalues the *cachet* of university education, as well as sacrificing quality to quantity.

Side by side with university expansion, the technical colleges — which had provided training in a wide range of professions, whether through full-time or sandwich and evening courses — were transformed into 'polytechnics', second-class universities providing a range of degrees as well as diplomas. Inevitably, the 'classless' Major Government gave them the title of universities. No-one was really deceived, though many people pretended to be.

Since the momentum for expansion is unstoppable, expansion has to be provided on the cheap. Funds for higher education have to be spread more thinly, disappointing everyone except the few institutions that have taken the initiative to raise their own funds. Student grants were pared and had to be supplemented by loans. Finally, tuition fees covering part of the course costs were introduced, thereby maximising dissatisfaction. Overstretched departments now farm out much of their teaching to inexperienced postgraduates. Often these are students who lack any teaching vocation, and have only stayed on to take a higher degree to defer the ugly moment when they have to make a living. There has been an inevitable decline in the quality of service to undergraduate students — just at the time when the government is asking them to make sacrifices in order to cover more of the cost of their courses.[7] It naturally follows that many students have begun to drop out — not necessarily because of any intellectual limitations, but often because they despise the meagre fare on offer. Thus the

[7]   Most university teachers now admit that they accept sub-standard students, and are reluctant to fail any of them in case their departments incur penalties; see *Times Higher Education Supplement*, 19 November 2004 [editor's note].

intention of giving higher education to all who might benefit
threatens to drive out those who would benefit most. Increasingly the universities will only seem attractive to the off-
spring of affluent parents who have yet to decide what to do
with themselves. Oblivious to the real plight of the universities, the Blair Government has promised to extend further
opportunities to the 'working class'. The Conservative Opposition has woken up to the absurdity of the 50 per cent target
for university entrants; but its enlightenment has arrived
much too late. It should have listened to the CPS in the 1980s.

A more successful group was our Trades Union Reform
Committee (TURC). In opposition, and the first year of government, trade union reform seemed to be among the least
likely objectives to be attained. James Prior, leader of the
anti-Thatcherite opposition inside the party, held that we
were in no position to fight the unions; where he and Heath
and the grandees had failed, no-one could succeed. He
believed that because he was on first-name terms with the
union leaders, there existed mutual understanding. His 'step
by step' approach was a euphemism for appeasement and
defeatism. The Department of Employment, which had long
since suffered agency-capture by the unions (like the media
industrial correspondents) backed him. Our group set out to
demolish his arguments and justify an active reform policy.

Our theoretical basis, developed from John Hoskyns's
'Stepping Stones'[8], was that the image of the unions had
changed for the worse, and that a 'Hobbesian' situation had
been created in which trade unionists, like other members of

[8]   For 'Stepping Stones', see John Hoskyns, *Just in Time: Inside the
       Thatcher Revolution*, Aurum Press, 2000, 39-65.

the public, suffered more from the actions of other unions than they gained from their own. They were more struck against than striking. This meant that policies which reined in the unions would be widely acceptable. We also questioned the claim of Prior and his officials that a majority of employers favoured step-by-step, and opposed stronger policies. We ascertained the actual views of employers, and were able to demonstrate that this was not the case. There was a majority in favour of action, so long as it was well thought-out and feasible. We were able to win Margaret Thatcher to our view. In due course, she exiled Prior to Ulster, promoting his protégés as a consolation prize, and brought in Norman Tebbit to see the legislation through.

Our campaign on union reform was helped by a group which was founded in 1980, during the Iron and Steel strike, to counter a serious effort by the union, backed by the Labour Party, to defeat economic reform by means of industrial action, thereby overturning the verdict of the general election. John Hoskyns and I feared that the steel-using industries would put pressure on the government to surrender, which would have been disastrous. We appealed to the CBI for support, but its leadership characteristically turned us down. I turned to Tom (now Lord) Boardman, a former MP and junior minister, then serving as President of the Association of British Chambers of Commerce, and active in Aims of Industry (AIMS), an organisation set up during the Second World War to oppose the drift towards socialism. He willingly offered his help, along with Mike Ivens, the director-general of AIMS. With the help of Walter Goldsmith, of the Institute of Directors, we mobilised a number of Trade Associations to form an action committee.

In naming the 'Argonauts' I thought of Jason confronted by the armed men who had sprung up when he sowed the dragon's teeth, and the stone he threw to get them fighting each other. Our main objectives were to persuade industry not to press the government to concede, to put some backbone into ministers, and to persuade trade unionists in steel-consuming industries, which outnumbered steel-producing industries by at least twenty to one, to put the interests of their industry and jobs above mythical trade union 'solidarity'.

During the early Thatcher years, the CPS was responsible for two further innovations. John Hoskyns and I had decided that the prime minister should have her own, independent economic adviser. I had invited the newly-appointed economic adviser to the Treasury, Professor Terry Burns, to lunch together with John Hoskyns. It struck both of us that though Burns's heart was doubtless in the right place, he was not sufficiently resolute to stand up to the Treasury team which was the guardian of neo-Keynesian orthodoxy. Moreover, located in Number Eleven, he had no incentive and limited opportunity to act as *advocatus diaboli*.

Mrs Thatcher was not necessarily convinced that she had been following wrong policies, but the virtue of having her own economic adviser instead of leaving her fate entirely in the hands of her Chancellor, Geoffrey Howe, made political sense to her. I decided on Professor Alan Walters, who had left Britain some years earlier for the USA. From a provincial working-class background, he had risen in academic life through a combination of intellectual distinction, originality and strong character in a field where the pressure to conform was intense. He had returned to deliver the annual Wincott

*Signed card presented to Sherman at a dinner
to mark his departure from the Centre for Policy Studies* ☞

FOUNDER ORDER OF THE GOLDEN FLEECE

PRESENTED TO ALFRED BY ARGONAUTS AND OTHER GOOD FRIENDS

"And now, therefore, after having been long on the way, we Argonauts of the ideal, our courage perhaps greater than our prudence, often shipwrecked and bruised, but, as I say, healthier than people would like to admit, dangerously healthy, recovering health again and again — it would seem as if our troubles were to be rewarded, as if we saw before us that undiscovered country, whose frontiers no one has yet seen ..."

— Friedrich Nietzsche, Ecce Homo

19.10.83

lecture, in which he expressed scepticism not only towards received ideas in economics but also the new government's policy of continuing Healey's IMF-imposed squeeze. His wife was known to prefer Washington, with its ostensibly classless lifestyle, and their grand house in Georgetown. But I persuaded him to agree to come if invited, then secured Mrs Thatcher's agreement that she needed advice and that Alan Walters was the man to provide it. Alan had, in fact, met Mrs Thatcher early in her career as Conservative leader, when I brought him with Paddy (now Lady Walters) to a couple of working dinners at my flat in Kensington. Years later, Paddy recalled how she had been struck at once by Mrs Thatcher's quick grasp and intellectual determination.

Alan stood out for complete independence from the Treasury and a high salary by the standards of the time — i.e. that of a Second Permanent Secretary (similar to that of Professor Burns at the Treasury) plus £20,000 per year, to be found by the CPS. This was not quite as much as it seemed. For one thing, salaries were (and are) much lower in the UK than in the USA. Secondly, temporary civil servants do not receive pension rights or compensation *in lieu*, which in the case of index-linked civil service pensions were reliably estimated as being worth more than 40 per cent on top of nominal salary. Thirdly, his income in the USA, where he held a Chair at Johns Hopkins University and was a departmental head at the World Bank, was considerably greater. He took up the new post in January 1981. I regarded this as a major contribution on my part. I arranged weekly off-record lunches for him with a wide variety of journalists, which over time expanded his authority.

Although the new government had continued his policies, Denis Healey denounced the squeeze as the product of 'Thatcher monetarism'. The epithet caught on, since few politicians or journalists had the slightest idea what monetarism meant, or what was at stake. The treatment of monetarism recalled Defoe's aphorism about the hundred thousand stout country fellows who would fight to the death against popery without knowing whether popery be a man or a horse.[9] In their turn, loyal Tories declared themselves to be monetarists, without a second thought. In spite of my own scepticism, I was dubbed a monetarist by hack journalists and politicians who were impervious to reason and depended on slogans as intellectual crutches.

I had economic problems very much in mind at the time of the CBI annual conference, in November 1980. The high pound, with its adverse effect on the balance of trade, was universally ascribed to the impact of North Sea oil. Michael Edwardes, of the subsidy-guzzling BL, was vigorously applauded when he denounced North Sea oil and suggested that they keep it in the ground.

I questioned this equation from the outset. For one thing, most petro-currencies tend to be weak, barely tradeable, whereas the major oil-importers had strong currencies – the US dollar, the Japanese yen, etc. I decided to commission some research. I persuaded the chairman of Taylor Woodrow, then also chairman of an employers' economic study unit, to subscribe £3,000, and obtained another £1,000 – half from David Wolfson. Since I could think of no-one in Britain

[9]   Quoted in William Hazlitt, 'Paragraphs on Prejudice', in P.P Howe (ed) *Complete Works* Dent, 1934, Volume XX, 328.

to whom I could entrust the study — otherwise they would have done it already — I rang Alan Walters in Washington, asking him to recommend someone to prepare a seminar paper for his guidance on arrival. He recommended two German monetary economists, then as an afterthought mentioned a Swiss-American, Professor Jurg Niehans. Currently at Berne, Neihans was a one-time adviser to the Swiss Central Bank, and was due to leave for the USA to keep Alan's chair at Johns Hopkins warm for the two years of his leave of absence in London.

I asked my secretary to try the Germans. She got no further than their secretaries, who spoke no English. I have no German. So I dialled directly to Neihans in Berne, speaking French. He came over, collected data, and in due course produced his report, ready for the seminar which I set up under Walters's chairmanship. There were participants from the Treasury, the Cabinet Office, the Central Policy Review Staff (CPRS), the Bank of England, and a number of individuals including Samuel Brittan. Neihans argued that the trajectory of government policy was broadly correct, but that its implementation had been faulty. He demonstrated that the excessive strength of sterling owed nothing to North Sea oil, but resulted from the neo-Keynesian monetary squeeze — both its intensity and the speed with which it had been imposed. He showed how in Switzerland some years previously, an excessively rapid squeeze had caused similar overshoot. He proposed a temporary relaxation of interest-rate policy followed by a moderate squeeze over a longer period.

Walters took the message on board, and it formed the basis for the budget of spring 1981. This was criticised by 364 economists — the priests of Baal — in a letter to the *Times*. But it proved to be the starting point for recovery.

The affair had some political fall-out whose significance I should have noted. Professor Hugh Thomas had been appointed chairman of the CPS after the 1979 election victory. His *Spanish Civil War* was widely translated and was regarded as the most authoritative work on the subject in Spain itself.[10] He had given up his academic post and become (in his words) an independent man of letters. I had met him previously while he was working on a study of Cuba (which I had visited and written about back in 1972). I reviewed his Spanish book when it appeared. I got in touch with him again in 1976, to ask whether he would help to provide some backing in Britain for an academic who had broken with the Spanish Socialist Party because it was too left-wing, and formed a Social-Democratic Party. In the event, Thomas informed me that he had been one of a group which had broken away from the Labour Party and now supported Margaret Thatcher, without any particular organisational framework. I introduced him to Mrs Thatcher, as a source on foreign policy in general and Central America in particular. I suggested that he should be considered as a future director of the Conservative Research Department. Mrs Thatcher agreed, and asked Keith Joseph to negotiate this with Lord Thorneycroft, the Party Chairman. However, Thorneycroft wanted to appoint his protégé, Alan Howarth, then his personal assistant, in order to bring Central Office and the CRD to heel (Howarth later achieved notoriety by crossing the floor and joining

---

[10] First published by Eyre & Spottiswode, 1961; numerous subsequent editions.

Labour, but in the late 1970s he was as Thatcherite as the next man). Joseph conceded, but Thomas was given the CPS chairmanship as a consolation.

This was awkward for me, because my position was effectively downgraded. Instead of dealing directly with Keith Joseph or Margaret Thatcher I was subordinated to a new chairman — an extra layer of authority, though I did continue directly to deal with Mrs Thatcher as an *ad hoc* speechwriter and adviser. I failed to recognise any other possible problems. But in 1981 Thomas, with whom I had previously enjoyed good relations, suddenly intervened to demand withdrawal of the Niehans seminar paper and to forbid its dissemination. The donors who had financed the study then asked for their money back, and Thomas was obliged to temporise. At the time, I feared that Mrs Thatcher might have been behind this. But I later learned that Walters had given her the results of the seminar and she had accepted them.

I did not feel at the time that I was being sidelined. In the spring of 1982, during the Falklands crisis, I phoned the prime minister on several occasions, pointing out the pitfalls of accepting the compromises which were being pressed on her by colleagues and by the US secretary of state Alexander Haig, who fancied himself as a great pacifier. It seemed ludicrous that one of the most powerful people in the world, with all the apparatus of the state at her disposal, should need an interlocutor of this kind. But during the conflict she received little encouragement from her colleagues — indeed it felt more like discouragement and opposition. Her main backing in Britain came from the Naval top brass, who were engaged in a life and death struggle with the RAF at the time, for a share of diminishing defence resources. The strong personal relationship between Thatcher and Reagan saved the day for her, overcoming influences like Jean Kirkpatrick, the US ambassador to the UN, whose Latin American specialism dominated her thinking. But at the height of the conflict Mrs Thatcher felt most isolated and most in need of support. Shortly after the victory, she suddenly turned to me at a reception and said, 'Never complain again that you don't have influence!'

Against this background, the subsequent bombshell was the more inexplicable. In the following year, a few days after the 1983 general election, I was summarily dismissed from the CPS and blacklisted. One of Mrs Thatcher's advisers told me afterwards that he doubted whether she knew herself why this happened. She was under pressure to get rid of me from a coalition, including grandees, ministers and other late- arriving hitch-hikers on the Thatcher bandwagon. Faced with this combination, she took the path of least resistance. I went to see her. Our conversation told me little about why a colleague who had been with her from the beginning — indeed, from before the beginning, supporting her loyally but frankly, and whose work she had praised not long before the event should be dropped and excluded. Earlier that year I had been recommended for a knighthood. That now looked like an attempt to console me for what was to come.

One or two crumbs of knowledge came to me. Early in 1982, Lord Weidenfeld, whom I had met at a lunch given by Hugh Thomas, had asked me to see him and proposed that I write a book. I declined; I am not a book-writing animal but a journalist and essayist, and in any case I was far too involved in my work. But apparently I was being accused of having signed a contract to write a book saying that Margaret

Marching Orders?

Thatcher had failed.[11] I checked up with Weidenfeld, who agreed with my version of the meeting, and added that he had invited me at Thomas's instigation.

Another suggestion is that a coterie which included the late Shirley Letwin had said that the CPS would be able to attract far more support from academics if I were excluded. But this leaves the question of why Mrs Thatcher, who was aware of my qualities and had incurred something of a debt over the years, should have accepted this view (which turned out to be ill-founded). Letwin, an American friend of Joseph, later published a book on Thatcherism in which she covered the train of events which brought about Thatcher's ascendancy without even mentioning my part, leaving the reader to assume that Keith Joseph had been guided by her and her academic friends.[12] It is a reminder that 'unpersonning' and perversion of history is not confined to Communists.

I was not the only early supporter to leave at around this time. John Hoskyns had resigned from the Downing Street Policy Unit at the end of April 1982, frustrated by civil service obstruction. Norman Strauss, who had been on a temporary secondment, had already gone. After the 1983 general election Alan Walters returned to the USA, although he came

[11] Ironically, John Hoskyns recalls a conversation with AS in March 1982, after Hoskyns' departure from the Downing Street Policy Unit. When Hoskyns asked AS if he should write a book, AS 'said emphatically yes. If I waited, and did a memoir much later, it would be too late to be any use': John Hoskyns, *Just in Time*, 375 [editor's note].

[12] Shirley Robin Letwin, *The Anatomy of Thatcherism*, Fontana, 1992. Letwin (whose son Oliver worked for Joseph before becoming a Conservative MP), only mentioned AS on one page of her long book [editor's note].

back to Britain later, with interesting consequences. It is not unusual for leaders to drop those who were with them from the outset, and surround themselves with dependents who tell them what they wish to hear. But in Mrs Thatcher's case I have reason to believe that this process was unconscious, at least in the early days.

As I have argued, the ideas associated with the CPS were never internalised by ministers, but co-existed with an inherited policy-making mind-set. Life was more comfortable for policy-makers when my dissenting voice was stilled, and the main CPS study groups disbanded (as they were after my departure).

The Thatcher 'revolution' began under the shadow of electoral considerations. 'We must compromise to win elections' continued to inhibit bolder analytical thinking even at the best of times. For example, criticism of the welfare state in light of history, logic and empirical evidence was ruled out. Terms like 'public services' were immune from criticism. The consideration that government intervention in housing has done more harm than good was excluded.

The widely-accepted myth that the early Thatcher regime was 'ideological', and that the government was later obliged by events to become 'pragmatic' (i.e. unreflective), obscures what actually happened. The dichotomy between Thatcherite (or, if you like, Shermanist) rhetoric and the mind-set which underlay policy-making started to grow as soon as the election was won. Against us was ranged not only the majority of the cabinet, party hierarchies, the CRD and the *nomenklatura*, but also the civil service, large sections of the media and economic vested interests on 'both sides of industry' and beyond. I do not know how we could have done better, given these circumstances and our scanty resources. Even the need to do so took time to sink in; like other people, we enjoyed the taste, smell and appearance of power, seated with the mighty.

Chapter 6

The Long Haul, 1983–90

The 1983 election marked a high point in Mrs Thatcher's leadership. She had begun to bring some order into the economic chaos which had been handed down from government to government, and had begun to stamp her personal authority on the Treasury's policies. She and her government — in that order — were taken seriously abroad; the special alliance with the United States was re-established as a buttress of the West. James Prior had been sent to Ulster, ending his threat to Mrs Thatcher's position and to her trade union reforms. Critics like Norman St-John Stevas and Sir Ian Gilmour had been dismissed to the backbenches. She felt in a position to commence 'Thatcherising' British society.

This represented an evolution in Conservative governance, from conserving towards accommodating and facilitating changes which had already been generated in the bowels of British society itself. True, the Conservative Party as a party of change had been a fact of life for generations, but it was not conceptualised as such. Now image became a more adequate reflection of reality.

Dropsical state expenditure and the tax-gobbling purposeless nationalised sector were now in her sights. European encroachment on British sovereignty was to be warded off, mass immigration controlled, welfare hypertrophy curbed. She had some victories on her way, sufficient to inspire her to greater efforts. But the Holy Grail was not for the taking.

To bring about and consolidate a revolution — call it a 'counter-revolution' if you will, it means the same thing — necessitates a revolutionary class. But the Conservative MPs, grandees, 'grey suits' and organisation men were far from revolutionary.

When John Hoskyns joined the CPS and tried to conduct seminars for the shadow cabinet, he was shocked by their lack of capacity for sequential thinking of cause and effect. They compared unfavourably with business executives he had worked with. The few radicals among the Conservative Party and its baggage-train, as we have seen, were not so much the New Right as the 'newly right'; mainly ex-socialists whose search for Utopia had led them to abandon socialism but not necessarily its ultimate objectives and certainly not its mindset. Despite the numerous 'conversions' in the mid- to late-1970s, most revolutionaries by temperament or conviction were still on the Left, seeking a diametrically different kind of revolution.

Before the 1979 general election I often worked from the opposition leader's office by day. It overlooked the statue of Queen Boudicca, driving her chariot, whipping her horses. As leader of the opposition and subsequently as prime minister, Mrs Thatcher actively whipped her horses in Boudicca style. But, although government was no longer as immobile as the statue, the effect of her promptings was limited. She would have needed a different breed to ride to her destination. Once again, in retrospect, I am bound to marvel at how much she achieved under the circumstances.

In British politics, most phenomena have their positive and negative aspects, cutting both ways. The collapse of the recently-powerful Labour Party into conflicting factions for the second time since the Second World War made life easier for the post-1983 government in some obvious ways. But it also mitigated some checks and balances which had shaped political life. No longer living on a knife-edge had its effects on the psychology of the parliamentary Conservative party, reinforcing earlier developments. There were far more 'professional' MPs — a majority, reversing the pattern of earlier days. Often these individuals began as student politicians and progressed as research assistants before eventually making it into the Commons, always toeing the line without ever making contact with the real world. Parliamentary salaries and other perquisites were insufficient to maintain a middle-class lifestyle. School fees were now much more important, as the average age of new Tory MPs fell, under Central Office pressures. MPs were drawn into 'consultancy', which came to mean trafficking in influence (real or imagined). With many Conservative MPs involved, standards of behaviour declined, along with the leadership's power to restore them even if it wished to do so. Loyalty was replaced by self-interested calculation, generating excessive sensitivity to opinion polls, and hence institutionalising short-termism and instability.[1]

Whereas Mrs Thatcher's successive election victories and high profile had built her support in the party outside Westminster, reaching something like an adoration which largely survived her downfall, they left the parliamentary party ambivalent. While appreciating her high profile and campaigning skills which had provided them with seats and the fruits of office — including those lucrative 'consultancies' — they feared her adventurousness and militancy. Seeing the opposition at sixes and sevens, they too easily forgot their tribulations in the 60s and 70s, and their vulnerability to ejection at the next swing of the pendulum. A majority still favoured Butlerite policies, in Heathite hands. They approved their government's adhesion to the EEC and were reconciled to a greater or lesser degree of Europeanisation. Under Thatcher (who had her misgivings) and Major (who had none) their Europhile zeal persisted, giving way to widespread Euro-scepticism only much later, after their crushing defeat.

After the 1983 election some of the excitement went out of Conservative politics. The Tories were no longer seen as 'the stupid party', but had yet to set their stamp on political thinking. Labour was clearly *hors de combat*, and would be for some time; its future as a major party was even questioned. The Social Democratic Party (SDP) was making the running in the intellectual sphere, and the Liberals were making headway with their street politics. Despite its setback at the 1983 gen-

---

[1]   On this point see also Mark Garnett, *The Snake that Swallowed its Tail*, Imprint Academic, 2004, chapter 3.

eral election, the Liberal–SDP Alliance seemed destined to displace Labour as the second party and the major threat to Conservative hegemony.

But nature abhors a vacuum. With Labour in turmoil and the Alliance still feeling its way into developing a positive political personality, effective opposition was left to the Churches, the civil service, academe, the media, celtic nationalism and the residual discontented in Conservative ranks.

Margaret Thatcher's confrontation with the unions was meeting continued success. Far from being seen as fighting the class war, or union-bashing, restrictions on 'industrial action' were increasingly accepted as enfranchisement of workers, employers and consumers alike. While not going so far as to reverse the easements granted during the early years of the century, the legislation brought in under Tebbit and his successors made it difficult for militants and union bureaucrats to bring workers out on strike against their will, and outlawed vexatious practices like secondary action. Perhaps the best testament to the legislation's fairness is its survival under two terms of a Labour government with a large majority, heavily indebted to union paymasters.

Concerted efforts were also made to roll back the tide of nationalisation. Gas, water, electricity — avatars of municipal socialism which had been nationalised after 1945 (to howls of Fabian and local government protest) — were privatised without much trouble. Whatever feelings of ownership or identification might conceivably have accrued to municipal enterprises had certainly not transferred to the nationalised services.

Grosso modo the process of privatisation was a success. True, management standards were low, and the newly-independent boards awarded themselves private sector salaries in advance of private sector performance. But it cut costs and worked. Telecommunications were liberated, just in time to accommodate the proliferation of mobile phones and fax machines. Margaret Thatcher had already nipped the state North Sea oil enterprise in the bud. Otherwise who knows whether this resource might not have exacted subsidies, instead of making profits — like coal, a former source of wealth-creation prior to nationalisation?[2]

In opposition, I had urged Mrs Thatcher to profit from the experience of the Tudor monarchs. After rejecting Papal authority, Henry VIII dissolved the monasteries, not only dispersing their monks ('mad' or otherwise) and hangers-on, but also selling off their property. This action had created new productive vested interests against the restoration of that property. He used some of the resources to found grammar schools in order to create a secular literate class, ending the clergy's monopoly of literacy and numeracy. Similarly, I argued that only rapid de-nationalisation and de-monopolisation would create vested interests which would rally behind the cause of a freer economy. But this line of argument was considered extreme. Perhaps so; but this was no reason to stumble into privatisation almost by accident, with a piecemeal, hand-to-mouth programme which lacked any strategic dimension.

---

[2]   Critics argued that oil revenues were indeed frittered away, in tax cuts for the already-affluent [editor's note].

To some extent, Conservative denationalisation satisfied my hope that the Thatcher Government could *induce* rather than *impose* change, by making it in people's interests. This was certainly true of council house sales, one of the government's greatest achievements. But in general, privatisation has turned out to be a mixed blessing. The nationalised public utilities were so wastefully run that even cack-handed monopolistic privatisation showed savings. But the original promise of turning state monopolies into free enterprises was not fulfilled, in part because the original impulse was adulterated by the desire to raise money from them to finance additional government expenditure while simultaneously cutting income tax. This was most easily and profitably done by the expedient of handing over their assets to private monopolies, instead of competitive market-driven producers controlled through agreed codes of practice, as in the USA. As a result, regulators with vast arbitrary powers had to be appointed.

The problems of the railways are popularly ascribed to privatisation, but they actually stem from the dysfunctional nature of rail itself. From the 1820s till the beginning of the twentieth century, rail revolutionised the transport of people and goods. It had three-quarters of a century's start on modern road transport, and was a further half century ahead of mass air travel.

But the combined effects of the internal combustion engine, the pneumatic tyre and road surfacing enhanced the competitive position of road as against rail. For leisure travel rail and other forms of public transport became broadly uncompetitive. Hence rail's share of passenger mileage had fallen from forty per cent in the 1955 traffic census to just eight per cent twenty-five years later.

But rail enjoyed powerful political and emotional support, expressed among other things in sizeable subsidies, while motor travel is heavily taxed. Both rail subsidies and petrol taxation are strongly regressive. But the subsidies, however heavy, are insufficient to finance a satisfactory service. Their effect, combined with the vast growth in state employment centred on the South East of England, is to generate a massive weekday tidal flow in and out of Central London and other major urban centres, to the discomfort of taxpayers and passengers alike.

Although the public blames the troubles of the network, including safety lapses, on privatisation, re-nationalisation is still unattractive to a Labour government which would thereby be saddled with vastly-increased expenditures. Even this would bring little consumer satisfaction to the highly-subsidised mainly middle-class minority of suburban rail-users. The dilemmas remain to plague Blair.

From Thatcher's election as leader in 1975 to 1984, the threat of a coal miners' strike — more properly described as an insurrection — hung over the heads of the Conservatives. With the menace of the cold war receding, the threat's magnitude was comparable to that posed by General Galtieri in 1982. She had to meet it and defeat it in order to rule in peace. Plans had been made in opposition to counter the threat, by a committee headed by Nicholas Ridley; the proposals for resolute resistance had been leaked by Christopher Patten in an attempt to pre-empt the action.

In the early years, Mrs Thatcher backed away from a confrontation. But the die was cast in the autumn of 1983, when the NUM President, Arthur Scargill, announced that since the Labour Party had failed to oust Mrs Thatcher by democratic means, the unions would do so instead.

Like the Falklands expedition, the strike was accompanied by serious risks which future generations may not automatically appreciate. Scargill's flying pickets, supported by much of organised labour, had twice defeated the Heath Government and gained the aura of invincibility. But Mrs Thatcher's position compared very favourably with that of Heath in his day. First, her defeat of Galtieri and successful earlier tussles with the unions earned her a degree of public confidence which Heath and his colleagues had never cemented. Second, the plans for conflict had been refined over several years. Third, the weak leadership of the National Coal Board (NCB), which had appeased the miners and even rehashed statistics to support their case, had been replaced by a robust industrialist, Iain MacGregor, who had already succeeded in reshaping the iron and steel industry after being head-hunted by Keith Joseph at the DTI. Finally, and most importantly, Scargill's over-confidence enticed him into calling a strike at the wrong time of year, when demand for coal was low.

As with the Falklands, Mrs Thatcher's resolution permeated and decided the process. It was a contest which brought out the prime minister's strengths. By making selective use of the Tebbit legislation, she was able to divide the miners, keeping the East Midlands coal-fields out of the strike. In this situation, the Home Secretary was bound to play a key role.

As chance would have it the Home Office was occupied by Leon Brittan, a clever lawyer but someone who was not

regarded as particularly strong. Early on, Mrs Thatcher read
the riot act to him, and he responded. Contrary to pessimistic
assumptions, the police responded magnificently to firm
leadership, and determinedly maintained the rule of law in
the face of organised violence.

In their previous strikes against Heath's Government, the
miners enjoyed full support from the Labour Party and the
trade unions, individually and collectively. This time the
reaction was mixed. Scargill's failure to bring the whole of his
own union behind him gave other TUC leaders room for
manoeuvre. The last thing they wanted was another situation
like the 1926 General Strike, with the general public largely
antagonistic.

After more than a year's struggle and some nail-biting
moments the strike collapsed. The opportunity to run down
the mining industry year by year eventuated, though it was
to take decades and further heavy expenditure to complete.
Once again, fortune had favoured the brave. But it was a
close-run thing.

At this point it is tempting to seek to identify the moment of
downturn, when Mrs Thatcher's triumphal career began to
turn sour and to herald her downfall. But it would be a fool's
errand. Just as we are said biologically to embark on the process of dying at the moment of birth, Mrs Thatcher's tribulations began to take shape when her star was at its zenith. Alan
Walters had returned to the US to safeguard his pensions.
Alan matched a strong intellect with personal resilience and a
belief in the legitimacy of logic, which had given a new
dimension to Mrs Thatcher's confrontation of economic haz-
ards. He turned out to be irreplaceable.

For my own part, I had been able to speak to her frankly though respectfully, a service which most leaders at most times stand most in need of. I had been dropped without explanation, and other candid counsellors had already taken their leave.

Some disparate factors combined to bring her down. Paradoxically, her increased power after winning her third election and thinning out the ranks of opponents — combined with a touch of hubris as she towered above survivors and newcomers — enabled her to push through the Community Charge, which earlier colleagues might have prevented. Secondly, her Bruges speech (September 1988), which expressed publicly for the first time her deep and growing misgivings about Europe, had dysfunctional political effects comparable with those of Enoch Powell's 'Rivers of Blood' speech two decades earlier. Its stark logic presented a challenge to Europhiles and Eurosceptics alike. Years later she was to spell out her misgivings more fully in her book *Statecraft*,[3] and show how adhesion to the EEC had launched Britain on a slippery slope, exacerbated by subsequent agreements.

But like Powell, she lacked a follow-through plan after the Bruges speech. Whether it would have been politically possible for her to turn Britain round would be an interesting exercise in speculation. But she did not attempt it, while her *Euromafiosi* opponents and enemies here and abroad took the speech as a wake-up call, and decided that the time had come to strike. So instead of a call to arms, the Bruges speech became the prelude to a swan-song.

[3] HarperCollins, 2002.

Her tiff with Michael Heseltine over the Westland affair
(1986) was an error of judgement. Heseltine's proposal that
the Westland helicopter firm should be sold to a European
consortium, rather than the American manufacturer Sikorsky,
deserved to be taken seriously. But she allowed personal feelings to cloud her judgement, and turn what was a legitimate
difference of opinion over a secondary matter into a personal
clash which in turned jogged Heseltine's ambitions into
motion. But even by that time several of her decisions and
actions manifested fatigue and isolation, having borne her
burdens for more than a decade.

Mrs Thatcher's downfall was accelerated by her efforts to
impose a bold solution to the problems of local government
finance through the ill-fated Community Charge. The issue
was a government Achilles heel from day one. I remember
Carol Thatcher chiding me shortly after her mother's election
as Conservative leader because I had rubbished a proposal to
consider the abolition of rates.

Labour's Richard Crossman had characteristically raised
and then dropped this idea in the mid sixties, proceeding
instead with a massive reorganisation of local government
which predictably raised costs and gave no benefits. When
Anthony Crosland inherited ministerial responsibility for
local government in the mid-1970s, he was appalled by its
wasteful levels of expenditure. In May 1975 he had the
Labour Party's annual local government conference raging at
him when he told them 'the party's over'. Nonetheless, the
party continued. Mrs Thatcher inherited a dysfunctional system. But with so many more pressing contents in her poi-
soned chalice she gave it low priority, underestimating its
politically lethal qualities.

Having served as a borough councillor and written on local government for the *Daily Telegraph*, I was in a position to disabuse her. On the first Christmas/New Year break after her election, she was kind enough to invite me with my family to Chequers, where among other things she claimed that Tom King, then Minister of State at Environment, had successfully elaborated procedures to solve the vexed problem of the Exchequer grant to local government. I was obliged to explain that the problem in its present form was insoluble, because expenditure and revenue-raising were unrelated. I remember adding that local government financial problems could not be solved at the revenue end only, but required a simultaneous solution of the revenue, expenditure and structure dimensions. That was in 1979–80. More pressing problems supervened. Things dragged on for several years, with local government spending rising and more authorities falling into Labour and Alliance hands while the Exchequer (ie business and household taxpayers) had to finance their profligacy. 'Rate-capping' powers taken by the government excited political opposition without relieving the taxpayer.

Local government's exactions had grown in tandem with the welfare state. The democratic pretensions of successive Representation of the People Acts, which turned ratepayer suffrage into universal suffrage, increased the proportion of local government expenditure funded from the Treasury and exposed the lack of checks on local authority spending. Central government had been slow to act against this problem, and it was essential that Mrs Thatcher should be more decisive since local government spending accounted for a high proportion of state expenditure. Twice I proposed to Conservative grandees that we should institute a government study of local nepotism and jobbery. But they turned this down, on the grounds that Conservatives in local government would object.

In the early eighties I planned a programme of studies into local government assets, with a view to their disposal. Due to decades of inflation, most were held on the books at a fraction of their original value. Many drew subsidies, few earned very much compared to their capital value. I took two examples: baths, and non-residential properties owned by housing departments (e.g shops). Municipal baths had originally been built when few working people had bathrooms; provision of facilities for regular baths was considered worthwhile on health grounds. Council schools sent children for a weekly bath. Then, in course of time, town centres were redeveloped and former inhabitants moved into council or private housing equipped with bathrooms. The council baths in the town centres became redundant and uneconomic. But the baths had staff and the council would have a baths sub- committee with a chairman and vice-chairman, who resisted closure. To safeguard their positions, councils provided temporary subsidies, which in course of time grew permanent and larger. Studies showed that in some councils, subsidies accounted for up to ninety per cent of baths' income. Closing down the baths would not only save subsidy (and repair) bills, but realise substantial capital gains from selling off town centre real estate. However, unless they were forced to do so by central government, councils had no incentive to carry out these reforms, whose beneficial financial effects could result in loss of Exchequer grants and other perverse subsidies.

Also, many council housing estates contained shops. In general they were badly administered, charging low rents and leaving little incentive to improvement. Run commercially, they would have brought much better returns, and could have been sold off to reduce council debt. But baths and shops on housing estates were only a small part of local government capital assets which could be sold off at profit, taking the strain off rates and also helping to invigorate urban economies.

This was a time when the Conservatives' prestige as the natural party of government was at its highest, and Labour's (under Michael Foot) at its lowest. I was therefore able to attract experts who were not necessarily Conservatives, but were happy to collaborate with the CPS in rethinking policies if there was a chance that their contributions would reach Downing Street. I put together a high-powered non-partisan group to undertake this task. It held its preliminary meeting just when my services as director of studies at the CPS and member of the leader's entourage were dispensed with. As a result, this study group, like the others, withered on the vine.

Then, after Mrs Thatcher's third successive election victory, nemesis loomed. A rating revaluation was due, arousing fears that it would wreak havoc. I was personally sceptical about this, on the grounds that the real dangers stemmed from expenditure levels, not the valuations themselves. But a mood of panic had set in, which permitted no second thoughts. Mrs Thatcher's response was the Community Charge, which came to be universally denigrated as the 'Poll Tax'. It was not as black as it was painted from the economic point of view, though it did suffer from logical flaws.

Its main shortcomings were political. It attempted to levy increased taxation on millions of lower-income householders without reference to services they were actually receiving, in the vain hope that this would somehow curb Labour and Liberal councils' profligacy. Its actual effects were predictable. First, it encouraged many councils to increase their expenditure. Second, it transferred the burden of all criticisms of profligacy from councils to the central government. Third, it gave the government's opponents of all parties common cause, while dividing its supporters, and antagonising Tory local government notables who carried weight in party affairs (although, ironically, their power had declined since the early 1980s because their numbers had been reduced by voters who punished them for the unpopularity of the Thatcher Government; had they been as influential in 1987 as they had been in 1979 the Poll Tax would almost certainly have been strangled at birth).

These shortcomings were obvious to observers irrespective of their politics. But Mrs Thatcher was curiously blind to them. Her legendary courage and determination, which had been an integral ingredient of her success and political longevity, worked against her. Her very strength turned out to generate a fatal weakness.

Her political opponents and personal enemies, inside the party and outside, remained hostile. As time went on, her position in the cabinet — her freedom of manoeuvre — actually weakened. Control of the cabinet and departments is not a once-and-for-all achievement, but must be renewed continually day by day, issue by issue. It entails personal loyalty and identity of views and interests. Harold Wilson compared government to a stage-coach, which must maintain momentum. It could also be compared to a continuous plebiscite.

Mrs Thatcher never enjoyed identity of views. She thrived on conflict, and conflicts grew around her. Friction between Norman Fowler's DHSS and Nigel Lawson's Treasury over reorganisation of the state pension arrangements was beyond Mrs Thatcher's power to mediate, and did her and the government real and lasting harm. She lost control of the Treasury, and allowed Lawson to get the bit between his teeth with loose monetary policies which sowed the seeds of inflation and a new cycle of 'stop-go'.

These developments had a curious history, characteristic of the vagaries of politics. During the 1984 party conference at Brighton, a year after the second election victory, Lawson was given a rough time from the floor for his consistent refusal to undertake monetary relaxation.[4] This was not the first call for a loosening of monetary restraint. But the weight of criticism fell on Lawson rather than her, as it had done in 1979–81.

The incident was overlooked at the time because of the bomb in Brighton's Grand Hotel, which almost killed the prime minister on the following morning. But Lawson drew his own conclusions, and began to relax monetary controls. Had Alan Walters still been at Number 10, he would have alerted her and proposed remedial action. But he was back in Washington, and I was out of the inner circle. So Lawson had a free hand.

---

[4]   Lawson attributed his poor reception to the fact that the speech 'was far too cerebral for a Party Conference and I delivered it in far too perfunctory a manner'; Nigel Lawson, *The View from No.11*, Bantam Press, 1992 [editor's note].

In its early stages, monetary relaxation brings feelings of well-being — live now, pay later! — so Lawson's popularity soared. His next conference speech was a triumph. When Mrs Thatcher was finally alerted to the situation, Lawson and his supporters fought back. At a meeting of the backbench 1922 Committee, MPs manifested their support, banging the lids of their desks. Lawson and cabinet colleagues further regressed from rationality by espousing membership of the European Exchange Rate Mechanism (ERM). By instituting fixed parities between European currencies the ERM was the harbinger of the euro.

Backed by Walters after his return to Britain, Mrs Thatcher opposed this move with arguments which accurately forecast the disasters leading up to 'Black Wednesday' in 1992. Nigel Lawson left the Treasury in 1989 without having taken Britain into the ERM.

But the policy persisted under his successor, John Major. Mrs Thatcher buckled under pressure from her colleagues and against her better judgement; she was no longer bolstered by Alan Walters, who had departed along with Lawson. It was a major retreat from the theory and practice of Thatcherism, and ineluctably sowed the seeds of post-Thatcher tribulations. Together with Conservative 'sleaze' and the reform of Labour's policies, it paved the way for defeat on an historic scale in 1997.

The events which led to the leadership election of 1990 and Mrs Thatcher's narrow defeat have been told and retold. Several caveats are required. She could have won the contest had she taken the threat seriously and fought back with her habitual vigour. She could be said to have been badly advised, or to have under-valued the importance of personal politics.

Had she spurned the bauble of the Paris celebration of the end of the cold war, and instead stayed in Westminster to meet MPs in singles and groups as she had done in 1975, she could have got through. The number of Thatcherite MPs who inadvertently spoiled their ballot papers by writing slogans of support on them, because no-one had warned them not to do so, would have been enough in theory to put her over the pass-mark. But in personal meetings she could have influenced several additional votes.

Back in office, she could have seen off Neil Kinnock at a general election, and handed over to a successor in time to escape the odium of 'Black Wednesday' which would have been blamed on the true culprits. She would have had no good reason for staying on further, because there was no Thatcherite successor to induct in any case. It was indeed an example of *après nous le deluge*.

Despite his enormous affection and respect for Mrs Thatcher, Keith Joseph was one of those who could have done more to help her survive in office. We had met rarely after 1983, though he attended a dinner given in my honour after I was dropped from the CPS and spoke in a highly complimentary fashion.

But a telling incident occurred around the time of the leadership challenge to Mrs Thatcher in 1990. My birthday is on November 10th, and the previous year he had attended a party at my home. I invited him again, only to be told that unfortunately he already had a dinner engagement for that evening, with friends.

On the morning of my party Joseph rang me to say that the *Evening Standard* had asked him to write them a leader-page feature article to appear the next day, but he had declined because of his dinner engagement. Given the seriousness of the situation, I was appalled by his seemingly cavalier attitude. However, he added that the *Standard* had agreed to take an article for the following Monday. Could I help him with this?

Naturally I agreed, and produced what I thought was a balanced and persuasive piece of the right length. Since the voting was obviously on a knife edge, a reasonable article by Keith Joseph might have swayed the balance. At my insistence, since I knew his habit of last-minute tampering, he undertook not to touch it without first consulting me. On Monday morning I went out to buy the *Evening Standard*, expecting to see my article. It was not there. Later that day, Joseph's secretary sent me, without explanation, an alternative draft he had written and sent without discussing it with me. It was largely taken up with an attack on Sir Geoffrey Howe.

As so often, Joseph had allowed his emotions to get the better of his judgement — as indeed Mrs Thatcher had done, by failing to conceal her evident contempt for Howe and thus provoking his acidic resignation statement in the Commons (13 November 1990).

Had she consulted Machiavelli, she would have sacked Howe in July 1989 rather than kicking him nominally upstairs into the functionless job of deputy prime minister and Leader of the House of Commons. There would have been some bitterness at the time, but he would have had no opportunity for a spectacular resignation — the only weapon he could use to satisfy his resentment.

As it turned out, he used Europe as the pretext for resignation when Mrs Thatcher was weakened by the public reaction to the unpopular Poll Tax. In November 1990, he gave additional proof that speeches can change history.

Chapter 7

The Legacies

Regimes, like individuals, have life-cycles. Mrs Thatcher had been swept into office at a time of crisis for the party and the nation, arousing great hopes in some quarters. But, in her turn, by 1990 she had come to represent a new status quo. Problems which had vexed the country when she bid for the leadership remained. The broad public, which had come to believe that the economic tribulations of the early Thatcher years had given away to a 'miracle' age of increasing prosperity, suddenly found itself plunged back into inflationary recession at the end of the eighties, with bankruptcies, lay-offs and the new scourge of negative equity and home repossessions. It was like the old days of 'stop–go', but the booms seemed to be getting shorter and less balmy, the busts longer and deeper.

Even her supporters felt that not enough had changed to justify their high hopes. It was not so much disillusion as a feeling of 'the morning after'. Some of the magic had dissipated. She had surfed the wave of populist feeling during her early years, less from calculation than from natural sympathies. By the time of the leadership contest she had fallen off it. The restive mood was reflected in widespread demonstrations against the Poll Tax.

The complexities of Thatcher's relationships with her cabinet and party have earlier and later parallels. Lloyd George may have been the first prime minister to feel that cabinet government constricted him, and hence that he needed instruments of his own. The 1922 Conservative revolt put an end to his innovations for the time being. Churchill experimented with 'overlords', supervising several departments, but this initiative was not sustained. Harold Macmillan attempted to work through the classical cabinet system, but he reversed this approach when he suddenly sacked half of his cabinet when things began to go wrong. Harold Wilson, trusting no-one, found the need to extend prime-ministerial power, and created the Downing Street Policy Unit which has since been institutionalised. Heath set up the Central Policy Review Staff (CPRS) to go some way towards transforming the Cabinet Office into a *de facto* prime minister's office. But departmental resistance nullified this development; the CPRS turned into a think tank which set its own remit, and was finally wound up by Mrs Thatcher.

The dilemma facing all twentieth-century premiers is whether to accept the division of powers between departments which have disparate objectives (and often political and personal objectives too) or to establish an over-riding governmental nucleus for decision-making. Mrs Thatcher was torn between the two. Her sense of propriety favoured the observation of classical divisions of authority, whereas practical considerations led to blurring at the edges by means of special cabinet committees. In the long run, this made less difference than critics would have us believe, since ministerial teams and their civil servants had powers of passive resistance.

In retrospect, Blair and Brown throw some light on what prime ministers (and co-premiers) can do within the loose limits of British constitutional practice, when they are so minded. Whether Margaret Thatcher could have 'done a Blair' or a 'Blair–Brown' is a matter of speculation. Part of the difference in their situations is that Blair came to office with the awful warning of the Foot–Kinnock years before his eyes and those of his party. Circumstances allowed him to structure the party's institutions to ensure his own domination. By contrast, Mrs Thatcher came to the party leadership trusting, even starry-eyed, humble in the presence of the Great and the Good, and only much later came to gauge its true character. Even then she made little complaint.

I recall an incident at a speech-writing session at one annual party conference. Someone had suggested paying a compliment to Whitelaw, her Deputy leader, praising him as 'wise'. 'He's not wise but shrewd', was Mrs Thatcher's immediate response. 'Shrewd' was an acceptable euphemism. Whitelaw never quite shrugged off the feeling that he should rightly have inherited the leadership, which he had lost as a price for refusing to stand against Heath in the first leadership ballot in 1975. His behaviour invariably suggested that the loyalty he owed to Mrs Thatcher had its natural limits. One example which comes to mind was the abolition of the Greater London Council (GLC) in 1985. Many Conservatives in local government opposed this, as was their right. But Whitelaw turned up at their meetings, shaking hands, patting backs and murmuring support. Of course, he could have argued that the future of London's government was an open question on which Conservatives had a right to take their own views. But what counted was the demonstration effect, unspoken but none the less cogent for that.[1]

Mrs Thatcher knew about Whitelaw's ambivalence, but she chose to suffer in silence. When his regular mishaps as Home Secretary made it essential to move him, she gave him a viscountcy (he had only daughters so the title lapsed at his death) and made him Leader of the Lords in place of the capable Baroness Young who thereby lost her place in the cabinet. This decision, perhaps, was compatible with political 'propriety'; but it reflected her general tendency to reserve her harshest decisions for her friends.

At some time in her political life — later than one might think — Mrs Thatcher lost her illusions, but not her idealism. In *Statecraft* she frankly confesses to early illusions in regard to the value of assurances given by the Eurocrats in return for the extension of their powers. This is the stuff of politics, which she would have anticipated had she taken my advice to read Machiavelli. She also spells out her second thoughts regarding Europe, arguing against the CAP and Common Fisheries Policy, and recommending a renegotiation which would be tantamount to exiting from the European Union, while advocating closer relations with the North Atlantic Free Trade Area (NAFTA). Though she goes much further

[1]   For an alternative interpretation of Whitelaw's motives and conduct, see Mark Garnett and Ian Aitken, *Splendid! Splendid! The Authorized Biography of Willie Whitelaw*, Jonathan Cape, 2002 [editor's note].

than the now mildly Eurosceptical official Tory line, she would have many takers for her views.

But whether it would have been possible for her to advance her idea from Downing Street remains a matter for speculation. *A propos*, Bernard Ingham, at the time Mrs Thatcher's spokesman, once referred to John (now Lord) Biffen as 'semi-detached', in a pejorative sense. But she could be said to have been semi-detached during the whole period of her leadership. Although she was at the pinnacle of power, many of the levers of power were not connected.

Consideration of the 'Thatcher interlude' throws up questions. First, could it have been any different? Could she have defeated fate and carried her revolution through? How different are things, for better or worse, from the state of affairs which would have prevailed had she not sought or gained the leadership? What legacy has she left? Was she the final dying flame of Tory radicalism? Why does she elicit more recognition (albeit grudging) from Labour leaders than from her own party, which seems to have decided that she is a non-person?

Having been close to the action for several years, I tend to the view that further study and reflection are needed, drawing on original documentary evidence and interviews to map the contours of events she helped to shape.

Thatcher as history and a lasting legacy is quite a different proposition from either the Joan of Arc figure or the ogre, though her personification in these contrasting ways is also part of the story. Disraeli and Gladstone's influence have survived them and shape our present-day thinking more than we would suppose. Thatcher will be judged by the same criteria. Yet we must also try to take the measure now because of its obvious relevance to contemporary political life, which is as full of twists and surprises as ever.

Her impact on events, both at the time and since, must be disentangled from her effect on the political culture, which is slower to take effect but may well be longer lasting. Margaret Thatcher can be classed together with Lloyd George and Attlee as political leaders who sought power with the express intention of changing society, and did so to the best of their ability.

Her impact was not as great as theirs, for better or worse, but she did leave a mark. However, whereas Lloyd Gorge and Attlee worked their way up to the leadership through a prolonged apprenticeship and were both well known for their views, Mrs Thatcher was parachuted into power from a relatively modest position as the result of unexpected events. Only after she had been exercising power and coming up against its limits, did her colleagues and opponents begin to acknowledge her qualities. But even then they were slow to understand her, because she was substantially different from them — a throw-back to the age of Peel and Gladstone, the age of missionary zeal, of puritan small-town society, of the Church militant.

In present-day Britain, Mrs Thatcher's impact on common political culture is substantial, but not immediately sensed. The changes she effected are taken for granted. When she was elected leader of her party, wage and price controls were the staple policies of both major parties. That particular will-o'-the-wisp had crippled several governments. Its hold on officialdom was strong. It has now disappeared from the political lexicon as a result of her endeavours. During Mrs

Thatcher's early years, 'monetarism' was denounced by socialists and many Conservatives alike as a deadly sin. Mrs Thatcher confronted this opposition frontally. The tenets which guided her are the new orthodoxy of both parties and of the Establishment in general. Monetary continence, once denounced as grinding the faces of the poor, is now *de rigeur*.

'Prudence', Gordon Brown's watchword, could have been Mrs Thatcher's, brought all the way from Grantham. She represented a transition from the age of interference to the age of working with the market. Here again, post-Thatcher practice is the most telling. The Labour government has eschewed vast ambitious schemes of nationalisation, economic planning, and subsidies for new claimants. Complaints by union spokesmen and Labour MPs, that their government is following the policies of its predecessors and even carrying them further, is the best testament possible to the formative impact of the Thatcher culture. The unions and the Labour Left may huff and puff, but can they blow the house down?

Fifty years ago, a Conservative MP of my acquaintance resigned his seat and left to work abroad on the grounds that the incumbent Conservative government was not turning back the clock but simply keeping the seat warm for Labour. Could the Blair–Brown Government by its acceptance of necessity be keeping the seat warm for a second round of Thatcherism?

Mrs Thatcher's fall from power was not only that of a person but of a personality. It is symptomatic that in the leadership election which followed her resignation, Michael Heseltine was beaten by John Major. Heseltine was a charismatic figure, tall, formed by Oxford and the Guards, a great platform and parliamentary orator, a self-made multimillionaire. His Europhile and modernising views were acceptable in 1990 to a majority of MPs. Yet they preferred Major, the epitome of Greyness, a machine politician who had been elevated by Thatcher and supported her bid for re-election. He generated no ideas or memorable phrases — apart from the ill-judged and counter-productive 'Back to Basics' — but was considered a safe pair of hands. It is difficult to avoid the conclusion that it was precisely his greyness as against Heseltine's flamboyance which decided the choice of many MPs. They had had enough of flamboyance, conviction politics and 'personalism' under Thatcher, and opted instead for a quiet life. Although Mrs Thatcher endorsed Major, her subsequent disillusionment with him was only surprising because the process took so long.

Mrs Thatcher's efforts to Thatcherise the Conservative Party never stood much chance of success. She remained a foreign body, and bred no successors to whom she could hand over the reins. The relationship between the leader and MPs is complex. A majority will have served under several leaders. Having seen them come and go, many expect to serve under several more. Insofar as it can influence the choice of constituency parties, the candidates' department of Conservative Central Office has always been a law unto itself — like the MPs it selects, it has watched the revolving door of leadership. Heath tried more than most to influence the choice of candidates, to ward off Eurosceptics or Powellites. Mrs Thatcher used her influence to secure seats for two ex-MPs, Jock Bruce-Gardyne and Teddy Taylor.[2] These efforts were resented. The main thrust of Central Office intervention has been to encourage the adoption of younger candidates, who tend to be 'professional' time-servers who are insensitive (or allergic) to ideas. The leader can work through the parliamentary whips, but much more on specific issues than on broader policy or philosophy; the whips can force MPs to vote, but not to think. Mrs Thatcher could address MPs from time to time at the 1922 committee, for what that was worth. For the rest, she could influence them only by the same means as she had to influence everyone else: through the fickle and distorting media.

Tony Blair's style of party management, and his relationship with the media, show that he has learned some of the lessons from the Thatcher interlude. In both respects, of course, he began with enormous advantages. By 1994 the Labour Party thought it was doomed to perpetual opposition, while in 1975 the Conservatives were merely stung because Harold Wilson had challenged their divine right to rule. Sections of the media were determined that Blair should succeed where previous Labour leaders had failed; and he came to terms with the rest. Academe, the Churches, the Establishment in the arts and sciences — all were predisposed to praise him. It was the model of a honeymoon, while most of Mrs Thatcher's senior colleagues had been hoping for a speedy divorce.

From this enviable position Blair has demonstrated the scope for a leader to interpret the logic of events according to his own criteria. He is one of the most personalist prime min-

[2] For the constituencies of Knutsford and Southend East respectively.

isters of modern times, leading from the front to an extent which only Lloyd George could match, and challenging his followers to unseat him or meekly follow. Time and again he has confounded prophecies of disaster. Of course, his luck might not hold and, before the time of his choosing, he may suffer the fate of most twentieth century leaders; politics is a cruel sport. But he could be said retrospectively to have validated Margaret Thatcher's boldness in outfacing her own parliamentary colleagues and seeking wider support.

But, returning to Ortega y Gasset's distinction, Blair seems to lack both ideas *and* beliefs, in so far as these can be made to inform a strategy for action rather than a recipe for re-election. His telegenic image may have swung votes, but he has not changed any minds. In particular, his actions in government have accelerated a loss of trust between the public and political leaders.

There is a populist mood abroad, which does not fit neatly into the hallowed Left–Right or liberal–conservative antitheses. Margaret Thatcher had too much respect for political proprieties to articulate this mood, at least not consistently and consciously; but part of her continued appeal arises from the sense that she *understood* it. Despite all the years of isolation in Downing Street, she never lost touch with her roots in Grantham. The world has changed significantly since her childhood; but the outlook persists. It is defensive and plebeian, anti-authority yet authoritarian. Recently it has been felt in Dianamania, the fuel-tax revolt, and the wide sympathy for Tony Martin, who shot dead an intruder in his farmhouse. It favours strong penal policies, and sees the common, law-abiding man as an underdog. It is reflected in changing attitudes to identity cards, which the public approves and distrusts by turns as the argument shifts from protection against fraud and violent crime to the preservation of traditional liberties. In the near future it might foment an upsurge of English nationalism. The English have watched with tolerance verging on indifference as the Scots and Welsh have been given a privileged constitutional position and a share of resources to match. But there is no certainty that this mood will not turn into resentment, and merge with opposition to absorption into a federal European Union. Then, almost anything might happen.

There is little hope that today's Conservative Party can articulate those views and channel them constructively. It is still suffering from a crisis of identity, a post-Thatcherite *anomie*. After her departure from office, one tendency within the party sought to huddle close to Labour on the 'middle ground', wherever Labour chose to locate it. While its critics accused New Labour of being Thatcher Mark II, many Conservatives were trying to become New Labour Mark II: to woo the public by finding out what it wanted and offering to give it to them. The minority sought to do the opposite and put 'clear blue water' between themselves and the opposition. As a result, whenever Labour shifted its ground, the two rival Tory phalanxes scuttled feverishly in opposite directions.

Having lost two elections and approaching a third defeat, the post-Thatcher Conservatives have the double challenge of presenting both an effective opposition and a credible alternative government. The two tasks are interlinked. Opposition without presenting an alternative has obvious dangers, since it all too easily entails adopting the government's agenda as a basis for judgement. This can end up in measuring how well the Labour government is performing by its own criteria, instead of moving the debate onto Conservative territory. At the time of writing (December 2004) the Conservatives are still groping towards the first stage, of becoming an effective opposition.

The Conservatives are suffering in part because they have yet to come to terms with their recent history. Their anxiety to turn their backs on the Thatcher interlude has left them unable to draw the appropriate lessons. With some indignation, they claim that they won the 'Battle of Ideas' in the 1970s and 1980s, only to have their clothes stolen by Labour. They fail to consider that the Battle of Ideas might not have been won in the first place; or rather, they are too ready to equate the collapse of the Soviet Bloc and Labour's rejection of doctrinaire socialism with a resounding victory for a coherent alternative philosophy. As we have seen, although an alternative view was available and Mrs Thatcher was ready to put it into practice, she was prevented from doing so. As I wrote soon after her departure from office, 'Too much was asked of her and too little help given — materially, intellectually, and politically'.[3]

Could the CPS and its allies outside parliament have tried harder to advance our critical views and win lasting acceptance for those alternative ideas? Given more resources, perhaps we might. The National Institute of Economic and Social Research, an Establishment body, had a staff of 45 principals and a budget to match. At the CPS, we had one or two principals plus a secretarial staff, with a modest budget for publications.

[3]   AS, 'The Fall of Thatcher', in *The World and I*, August 1991.

Could the media and political class have absorbed more 'Thatcherism' had we been in a position to supply it? The like-minded Institute of Economic Affairs was much larger and better funded than we were, and maintained a high rate of intellectually-respectable and challenging publications, lectures and seminars for decades, in addition to supporting the international Mont Pelerin Society and pioneering the independent University of Buckingham. But the time-scale of its operation and quest for influence is different from that of the CPS. The Institute of Directors was well-funded and militant. The Confederation of British Industries evolved considerably from its corporatist past, and ceased to be an antagonist of the IEA and the IoD. In many ways, the centre of gravity shifted further in the CBI than in the Conservative Party itself.

Distinctive Conservative criteria must now be adduced afresh for the twenty-first century. The Thatcher experience must be taken into account in this endeavour. The task entails a vision of Britain, just as Mrs Thatcher brought her vision with her from Grantham. It will have to confront the national question (or questions), relations between ethnically diverse communities, with the EU, the USA and the Commonwealth, the role of Christianity, etc. It will require a reassessment of human nature, the roots of crime and social breakdown, the scope and limits of market-oriented economics and of government action in society.

When Keith Joseph, Margaret Thatcher and I set out to challenge the post-war consensus in 1974 with the maxim 'thinking the unthinkable, questioning the unquestioned', we generated considerable momentum. The time is right for a second round of the contest.

Appendix

Speech by Sir Keith Joseph at Upminster, June 22 1974

Of course it is right that we should react strongly against Mr Benn's proposals to turn us into a nation of lame ducks.[1] Mr Heath's formidable speech on Thursday exposed the dangers. But it is not enough just to stave off Benn's preposterous proposals. The question we must all ask ourselves is how Mr. Benn was able to come within striking distance of the very heart of our economic life in the first place. How could it come about that the suggestions could even be made by a Minister of the Crown after a generation's experience of state ownership of a fifth of our economy? How could anyone expect that the idea of 'more of

---

[1] In the White Paper, *The Regeneration of British Industry*, the Industry Secretary, Tony Benn, had proposed to set up a National Enterprise Board (NEB) with a remit to take parts of British industry into public ownership.

the same' which has nearly brought us to our knees could be seriously entertained?

We must find a satisfactory answer to these questions if we are really concerned with our survival as a free and prosperous nation.

Of course, there is more than one answer. But an important part of the answer must be that our industry, economic life and society have been so debilitated by 30 years of Socialistic fashions that their very weakness tempts further inroads. The path to Benn is paved with 30 years of interventions: 30 years of good intentions: 30 years of disappointments. These have led the collectivists to say that we are failing only because we are taking half measures. The reality is that for 30 years the private sector of our economy has been forced to work with one hand tied behinds its back by government and unions. Socialist measures and Socialist legacies have weakened free enterprise — and yet it is Socialists who complain that its performance is not good enough.

If we simply stave off Benn and carry on as before, I fear that we shall have more disappointments — and more assaults. We must work towards the conditions in which the private sector — free enterprise — can realise its full potential for the benefit of all. Only then can it create the well-being which alone will buttress its political standing and preclude further assaults of this kind.

There is no good reason why this country should continue to fail. We have ample talent, the same kind of talent that made Britain great and prosperous a hundred years ago, the envy of the world. We enjoy the objective conditions for success as we did then.

Too much Socialism

This is no time to be mealy-mouthed. Since the end of the Second World War we have had altogether too much Socialism. There is no point in my trying to evade what everybody knows. For half of that 30 years Conservative Governments, for understandable reasons, did not consider it practicable to reverse the vast bulk of the accumulating detritus of Socialism which on each occasion they found when they returned to office. So we tried to build on its uncertain foundations instead. Socialist measures and Socialist attitudes have been very pervasive.

I must take my share of the blame for following too many of the fashions.

We are now more Socialist in many ways than any other developed country outside the Communist bloc — in the size of the public sector,[2] the range of controls and the telescoping of net income.

Comparison with our neighbours

And what is the result? Compare our position today with that of our neighbours in north west Europe — Germany, Sweden, Holland, France. They are no more talented than we are. Yet, compared with them, we have the longest working hours, the lowest pay and the lowest productivity per head. We have the highest taxes and the lowest investment. We have the least prosperity, the most poor and the lowest pensions. We have the largest nationalised sector and the worst

[2] In 1973 UK government expenditure (central and local government combined) was £30.342 billion; 54 per cent of net national income at factor costs.

labour troubles. Our education, our social services, our health services — our cultivated barbarisms — all give cause for concern. We find it more difficult than our neighbours to give the right treatment to the disabled and good rewards to such groups as teachers and nurses.

Moreover, unlike our neighbours we are and for some years have been a disinvesting nation. In real terms, we are consuming our capital stock faster than we replace it — our physical capital and our moral capital, the values built up and transmitted over generations. We have been eating the seed corn, neglecting our shrines.

True, some of the countries whose performance I have compared favourably to ours have been governed, at least partly or part of the time, by Social-Democratic parties. But the fact is that some Social-Democrat parties abroad are far more realistic in relation to private enterprise, to the essentials of economic policy, to the limits on government's power to intervene for good, than we here have been sometimes.[3]

The lessons for us

Mr. Benn's new offensive should make us pause to think. But in the event, re-thinking has begun anyway. I have been entrusted by Mr. Heath with drawing lessons from the relative success of these countries. To enable me to do this on the scale and depth the subject deserves, I am setting up a small policy study centre.

---

[3] This rather lame phrasing suggests that Joseph and Sherman preferred not to look too closely at the relative success of a heavily taxed neighbour like Sweden (editor's note).

I hope that in the months to come we shall be producing a flow of papers and presentations, which will deal comparatively and analytically with various features of our economies.[4]

But there is another instructive contrast — between the position as I have described it and our own good intentions. No one intended the present state of affairs to come about. Never in the course of this nation's history have so many good intentions by so many people created so many disappointments.

Then, what has gone wrong? I suggest four main answers.

Short cuts to Utopia

First, for the past 30 years, in our party-competitive efforts to improve life, we have overburdened the economy. We have over-estimated the power of government to do more and more for more and more people, to re-shape the economy and indeed human society, according to blueprints. We have tried to take short cuts to Utopia. But, for lack of a really good map, because we were in too much of a hurry, we have finished up further away than ever. In the social services, alas,

---

[4]   In fact, the CPS produced little insight into the contrast between the UK and other European countries, despite what was claimed to be its original remit. Although Sherman argues that the CPS simply lacked the resources to undertake a rigorous survey of European practice, it seems more likely that continental practice would uncover some unpalatable evidence about the co-existence of prosperous private enterprise and heavy taxation with a progressive purpose; see Denham and Garnett, *Joseph*, 240-3 [editor's note].

we seem to have generated more problems than we have solved. I was very conscious of this when I was the Minister.

We have found it harder than our neighbours to keep the overall level of demand — so important to the economy and to society as a whole — at about the right pitch. Too low — and labour is wasted: too high, when we try to mop up the last pockets of unemployment amid labour-shortage — and inflation is the result.

Not only have we most of the time over-burdened the economy but for 30 years industry has been distracted and harassed by constant and often unpredictable changes in policy and taxation and in the framework within which business has to operate.

During 30 years we have tried to force the pace of growth. Growth is welcome, but we just do not know how to accelerate its pace. Perhaps faster growth, like happiness, should not be a prime target but only a by-product of other policies.

The lean kine

Secondly, for 30 years, levels of state expenditure have been greater than the economy could bear. The private sector, the productive sector, has been weighed down by the burden of taxation, by the burden of subsidies to nationalized industries. The public sector has been draining away the wealth created by the private sector — labour, capital and management together.

We have achieved what seemed impossible. We have poured never-ending flows of real resources unto coal, rail and shipbuilding, among others, yet after 30 years they are as ailing and problematic as ever. We want healthy, well-paid, self-sufficient industries — giving good service to the public. Despite huge spending we still do not have them.

These are the lean kine which, as in Pharaoh's dream, are eating the healthy cows — the productive sector of the economy — and yet remain as hungry as ever. For 30 years we have tried to buy social peace at the expense of economic efficiency; predictably, we have got the worst of all worlds, inefficiency, hence poor performance and hence social discontents.

We can all write a list of public expenditure which we would call in question. Has it been wise, for example, to devote taxpayers' money to tourism — putting hotels before homes? Has it been wise to pour money and skilled people and growth firms — all needed desperately in our big cities — into new towns? Has it been wise to expand our universities quite so fast? There are many other forms of expenditure which need to be re-examined. They all placed burdens on free enterprise — the only creators of the resources we need for general prosperity.

I fought my colleagues hard for extra resources. But when we place too heavy a burden on the private sector, we stall the engine.

Trade Unions

Third, there are the trade unions. Workers here seem to co-operate less in creating prosperity for themselves than do the workers of north-west Europe. Our shop stewards and those they lead tend to be more resistant to change, less ready to improve techniques and more prone to strike, more given to damaging wage claims, than workers in north-west Europe.

The reasons go back deep into social history. As Tories we have to understand that we are dealing with real people with their own views, habits and prejudices. We certainly do not ask them to neglect their own self-interest. But we do invite them to transmute it into enlightened self-interest as their colleagues abroad have done. We must show that it is in flourishing profitable private firms that they can earn the most in the best conditions.

The Socialist vendetta

And fourth is the running vendetta conducted by the Socialists against our free enterprise system and those who manage it. Throughout the years a large section of the Socialist leadership has been downright antagonistic towards our wealth producers and towards the industry — national and multinational, large and small — which provides so high a proportion of our jobs, our exports and our tax revenue.

They have condemned the profit motive and attacked profits indiscriminately though for years profits have been too low for industrial health.

Indeed profits are the source of economic progress and, through their linkage with investment, of increased earnings and social services. Low profits today mean low earnings and low pensions tomorrow.

Profits earned within the law and in competition are thoroughly to be welcomed. But this has not been Labour's attitude over the years. A football team could not perform at its best if it were treated in the way that Socialists have treated British management.

It is pointless to argue about the level of investment when existing investment cannot be used properly because of poor labour relations, inflation, unpredictability created by continually changing government expedients. It is the quality and direction of investment that counts. We have destroyed or are destroying the market criteria for investment and production and have yet to produce another set.

These are the four main reasons why, in my view, things have gone wrong.

There are other reasons, too. Rent controls and local authority housing have almost destroyed the ability of people to move. Our well-intentioned social workers and misguided left-wing teachers have between them helped to erode the will to work.

Public opinion and prosperity

I do not believe that our neighbours in north-west Europe suffer the same difficulties. Trades unions, governments and public opinion understand to a greater degree than here the value of thriving private enterprise and provide therefore a more sympathetic and workable climate in which it can operate.

This much we can already learn from one or more of them: that poverty is not ended by levelling down; that great prosperity has no link with public ownership; that high earnings are bred by co-operation not by conflict.

It was Schumpeter who said that free enterprise would die only because it would by its very success lack defenders.

How absurd it would be if now, with the success of private enterprise and the failures of any alternative exposed before our eyes, we were to allow fashionable Socialism to continue to impose its prejudices.

We have inherited a mixed economy which has become increasingly muddled, as we tried our best to make semi-Socialism work. Its inherent contradictions are intractable. Judging from the past 30 years and paraphrasing Lincoln we have to ask 'can a country prosper, half collectivist, half free?' Certainly we couldn't prosper if we were even more collectivized.

The only practicable basis for prosperity is healthy, competitive free enterprise — a market economy within a framework of humane laws and institutions.

We must decide whether to go down with Benn or on to a more rational economy.

It is the Conservatives' job to try to bring about conditions in which free enterprise can carry the country and its standard of life and of social services forward to the levels that others nearby are enjoying.

We have the big task of opening the public's eyes to what is practicable. Governments are only free to act within the constraints set by public opinion. It is my job and the job of the Centre for Policy Studies now being set up to show what can be done, indeed what has been done, in nearby humane societies.

Bibliography

Cockett, Richard, *Thinking the Unthinkable: Think-tanks and the economic counter-revolution 1931-1983*, HarperCollins, 1994.

Conservative Central Office, *The Right Approach: A statement of Conservative aims*, 1976.

Denham, Andrew and Garnett, Mark, *Keith Joseph: A life*, Acumen, 2001.

Department of Industry, *Regeneration of British Industry*, Cmnd.5710, HMSO, 1974.

Dobson, Andrew, *An Introduction to the Politics and Philosophy of José Ortega y Gasset*, Cambridge University Press, 1989.

Frazer, James, *The Golden Bough* (1890), Canongate, 2004.

Garnett, Mark, *The Snake that Swallowed its Tail*, Imprint Academic, 2004.

Garnett, Mark and Aitken, Ian, *Splendid! Splendid! The authorized biography of Willie Whitelaw*, Jonathan Cape, 2002.

Garnett, Mark and Weight, Richard, *Modern British History: The essential A-Z guide*, Pimlico, 2004.

Gasset, Ortega y, *Meditaciones del Quijote* (1914) [*Meditations on Quixote*, Norton, 1984].

Gasset, Ortega y, *Ideas y creencias* [*Ideas and Beliefs*], Espace Calpe, 1940.

Hames, Tim and Feasey, Richard, 'Anglo-American think tanks under Reagan and Thatcher', in Andrew Adonis and Tim Hames (eds) *A Conservative Revolution? The Thatcher-Reagan decade in perspective*, Manchester University Press, 1994.

Hazlett, William, 'Paragraphs on Prejudice', in P.P, Howe (ed) *Complete Works*, Dent, 1934.

Hazlitt, William, 'On Good Nature', *The Round Table*, Everyman's edition, 1936.

Hoskyns, John, *Just in Time: Inside the Thatcher revolution*, Aurum Press, 2000.

Howe, Geoffrey, *The right approach to the economy*, Conservative Central Office, 1977.

Howe, Geoffrey, *Conflict of Loyalty*, Macmillan, 1994.

Joseph, Keith, *Reversing the Trend*, Centre for Policy Studies, 1975.

Joseph, Keith, *Monetarism is Not Enough*, Centre for Policy Studies, 1976.

Joseph, Keith, 'Stepping Stones to Power', in *The First Ten Years: A perspective of the Conservative era that began in 1979*, Conservative Central Office, 1989.

Lawson, Nigel, *The View from No.11*, Bantam Press, 1992.

Letwin, Shirley Robin, *The Anatomy of Thatcherism*, Fontana, 1992.

Morgan, Kenneth O., *Callaghan: A Life*, Oxford University Press, 1997.

Ranelagh, John, *Thatcher's People: An insider's account of the politics, the power and the personalities*, HarperCollins, 1991.

Rogally, Joe, *Grunwick*, Penguin, 1977.

Thatcher, Margaret, *Let Our Children Grow Tall: Selected speeches 1975-1977*, Centre for Policy Studies, 1977.

Thatcher, Margaret, *The Path to Power*, HarperCollins, 1995.

Thatcher, Margaret, *Statecraft*, HarperCollins, 2002.

Thomas, Hugh, *The Spanish Civil War*, Eyre and Spottiswode, 1961.

Urban, George, *Diplomacy and Disillusion at the Court of Margaret Thatcher*, I.B Taurus, 1996.

Young, Hugo, *One of Us: A biography of Margaret Thatcher*, Pan, 1990 edition.

Zweig, Ferdynand, *The Worker in an Affluent Society*, Heinemann, 1961.

Index

A

Adam Smith Institute (ASI), 30
Attlee, Clement, 73, 152

B

Bacon, Sir Francis, 16
Baldwin, Stanley, 22, 23
Benn, Tony, 96, 101, 163 and note, 162, 164
Bevin, Ernest, 74
Biffen, John, 151
Bismarck, Otto von, 65
Blair, Tony, 41, 59, 100, 104 and note, 110, 132, 149, 153, 155-6
Boardman, Tom, 111
Bonar Law, Andrew, 25
British Leyland (BL), 100-101, 104, 105, 115
Brittan, Leon, 133-34
Brittan, Samuel, 116
Brown, Gordon, 104, 149, 153
Bruce-Gardyne, Jock, 155